HEINEMANN HISTORY

RUSSIA
1917–1945

CLARE BAKER

HEINEMANN
EDUCATIONAL

Heinemann Educational,
a division of Heinemann Educational Books Ltd,
Halley Court, Jordan Hill, Oxford OX2 8EJ

OXFORD LONDON EDINBURGH
MELBOURNE SYDNEY AUKLAND
IBADAN NAIROBI GABORONE HARARE
KINGSTON PORTSMOUTH NH (USA)
SINGAPORE MADRID BOLOGNA ATHENS

First published 1990

British Library Cataloguing in Publication Data

Baker, Clare
  1. Soviet Union, 1917–45
  I. Title
  947.08

ISBN 0-435-31037-2

Produced by
Visual Image, Street, Somerset

Printed in Great Britain by Scotprint, Edinburgh

Acknowledgements

The author and publisher would like to thank the following for
permission to reproduce photographs where indicated:

The Bettmann Archive: 2.4D, 4.1F, 4.6B;
Camera Press Ltd: 2.1A;
Centre for the Study of Cartoons and Caricature: 5.2A and B;
Mary Evans Picture Library: 1.3F;
J. R. Freemann: 1.4C;
Hulton-Deutsch: 3.3B, 4.3D, 5.4A;
Illustrated London News Picture Library: 1.2A;
David King Collection: 2.1C, 2.2D, 2.3D and E, 3.1F, 3.2D and E,
3.4A and B, 3.5E, 4.2A, 4.4C, 4.6G, 4.7A, B and D, 5.3A and C, 5.5C,
F and G;
Novosti Press Agency: 1.1B, 1.5A, 1.6C, 2.6B, 3.2B, 3.3A, and D,
3.5A, 4.3B, and C, 4.5C, 5.3B, 5.4C;
Popperfoto: 1.3B, 1.5B, 2.5A, 3.1A, 3.2C, 4.5A, 5.5B;
Society for Cultural Relations with the USSR: 1.1A, 1.7D, 4.4H and I
Staatsbibliothek: 2.5E;
Topham Picture Source: 2.4A and B.

Cover photo from the David King Collection.

Many thanks to John Taylor for permission to reproduce the stamps
on page 17.

Details of Written Sources

In some sources the wording or sentence structure has been
simplified to make sure that the source is accessible.

Alexander Barmine, *One Who Survived*, Putnam, NY, 1945: 2.4E
Elizabeth Campling, *The Russian Revolution*, Dryad Press Ltd, 1986:
1.2E, 1.3C, 1.4A, 1.6D, 2.5B and C
Robert Conquest, *The Great Terror: Stalin's Purge of the Thirties*,
Macmillan, 1968: 4.2B
Isaac Deutscher, *Stalin*, Penguin, 1970: 1.7B
Deutscher & King, *The Great Purges*, Blackwell, 1984: 3.5F, 4.5D,
4.6B, C, D, F, G, H, I and J, 4.7C, 5.5B, C and D
Eugenia Ginzburg, *Into the Whirlwind*, Collins/Harvill Press, 1981:
4.2C
Andrei Gromyko, *Memories*, Hutchinson, 1989: 5.2C
Maurice Hindus, *Red Bread*, Jonathan Cape, 1934: 3.5C and D
Adolf Hitler, *Mein Kampf* (1924 trans. Ralph Manheim), Sentry
Paperbacks, 1943: 5.1A
Tony Howarth, *Twentieth Century History: The World since 1900*,
Longman, 1979: 2.2B, 2.3B, 4.1A
V. Kravchenko, *I Chose Freedom: The Personal and Political Life of a
Soviet Official*, Robert Hale Ltd, 1932: 4.1E and B
Dr Benjamin Lee, 'On Standing Up and Being Counted', from *The
Lancet*, June 1983: 4.2F
Lenin, *Collected Works*, vol. 45, Nov. 1920-March 1923, Lawrence
and Wishart, 1970: 3.1C, D and E
Philip Longworth, *The Cossacks*, Constable, 1969: 2.5D
Roger Pethybridge, *Witnesses of the Russian Revolution*, Allen &
Unwin, 1964: 1.3A, 1.6A, C, E, and F, 1.7C, 2.2A and C, 2.3A
Tamara Pimlott, *Stalin's Russia*, Macmillan Educational, 1984: 3.5B,
4.2D
John Reed, *Ten Days That Shook the World*, Martin Lawrence, 1926:
1.4B, 1.5C
E. M. Roberts, *Lenin and the Downfall of Tsarist Russia*, Methuen,
1966: 1.2B, 1.3E
Harrison E. Salisbury, *Russia in Revolution 1900-1930*, Deutsch, 1978:
1.3D, 2.1B
Victor Serge, *Memoirs of a Revolutionary, 1901-41*, 1963: 2.2A, 4.1G
J. Scott, *Behind the Urals*, Houghton Mifflin, 1942: 3.3C, 4.4B and C
M. Sholokov, *Virgin Soil Upturned*, Putnam, 1931: 4.1B
Alexander Solzhenitsyn, *The Gulag Archipelago*, Harvill Press, 1974:
4.2E
Stalin, *Selected Writings*, The Greenwood Press, 1942: 4.3A, 4.4A,
5.4B
Trotsky, *History of the Russian Revolution*, Pluto, 1977: 1.2D
Trotsky, *My Life: An Attempt at an Autobiography*, Pathfinder, 1970:
2.4C

CONTENTS

1.1 THE RUSSIAN EMPIRE BEFORE 1917

The Tsarist government

The Russian Empire was an **autocratic** state, that is, it was ruled by one man, the Tsar. The way the country was governed depended almost entirely on his personality. **Nicholas II** became Tsar in 1894. He was determined to keep his autocratic powers.

The Imperial Family lived in the Winter Palace in St Petersburg, surrounded by aristocrats, army officers and important government officials. They were not aware of the sufferings of the people.

Russian society

Most of the people in the Russian Empire were peasants. For centuries they had been tied to their landowners as serfs. Although in theory they had been freed from this slavery, in fact their conditions had hardly changed. Most peasants had no rights and did not own the land they worked on. The peasants were very poor, had few possessions and lived in very simple accommodation.

During the years 1890-1914 industry expanded in the Russian Empire. There was a great movement of people from the country to the towns. Working conditions in the towns were often extremely bad. The few efforts that the government did make to control factory life were largely ignored by factory owners. Wages were very low and the accident rate at work was very high. Living conditions for the industrial workers were as bad as those for the peasants in the countryside – many lived in huge barracks attached to factories. Some families even lived in the factories.

Despite all the hardship, most working people did not hate the Tsar. They saw him as a father-figure, who would help them if only he realized how they were being treated by evil landlords and factory owners. In 1905 many peasants carried Nicholas's portrait when they marched to protest about low wages and poor living conditions. When the troops guarding the Winter Palace opened fire on the peaceful demonstrators, the long tradition of a special 'family relationship' between the Tsar and his people ended.

Political opposition to the Tsars

Since the mid-nineteenth century a number of groups or parties had formed which were hostile to the Tsar. These groups were different in many ways. Some were secret, others were open. Some wanted to change things by using the law, others believed they must break the law to get what they wanted. They all disagreed about what should replace the existing system.

The ideas and writings of **Karl Marx** influenced the ideas of one of the more radical parties, the **Social Democrats**. Marx thought that industrialization would lead to society being ruled by the **bourgeoisie** (middle classes). The bourgeoisie made profits by selling goods made by the **proletariat** (working classes). There would always be a conflict of interest between the two classes which Marx called the **class struggle**. The class struggle would lead to a revolution where the workers would replace **capitalism** (where factories and land are privately owned) with a communist state (where factories and land are owned by everybody). Marx believed that a country had to have

SOURCE **A**

A workers' barracks in 1905.

SOURCE **B**

advanced industries and a working class interested in politics before this revolution could take place. Russia had neither. In 1903 the Social Democratic Party split over the best way to organize opposition to the Tsar. One section, the **Mensheviks**, were a revolutionary party waiting for support from the workers. The **Bolsheviks** wanted a smaller, more highly organized, party to lead a revolution.

There were two other important groups in 1917. The **Socialist Revolutionaries** were popular with the peasants. They promised to **nationalize** (take into state ownership) land and industry after the revolution. Finally, the **Cadets** represented a mixture of middle-class conservatives and liberals. They wanted the government to be more like those in Western Europe, and did not like the radical ideas of the other parties.

Russia and the First World War

In 1914 Russia entered the war against Germany and Austria-Hungary. At first the war was popular and support for the Tsar was strong. However, the war never went well for Russia. In 1914 the Russian invasion of eastern Germany failed and in 1915 Russia itself was invaded. In 1916 the Russian army began an offensive against the Austrians in the south. This was successful at first, but eventually the Germans came to help the Austrians. Over 1 million Russians were killed, wounded, or missing, and no land was gained.

The huge Russian army was mismanaged, and badly trained and equipped. Soldiers were treated without respect, and classified as second-class citizens. Ordinary soldiers were sickened by the enormous numbers killed on the battlefield, and their loyalty to the Tsar's cause was gradually shaken. Rather than defend the old regime as they had during the 1905 revolution, many were now ready to join, and if necessary to lead, a protest against the ruling classes.

Civilians also suffered during the war. Peasants could not sell what they grew because there was not enough transport to take it to the towns. Their precious livestock could also be taken from them. In the towns people suffered severe food shortages and were forced to work longer hours for less money. Even some nobles were angered by the Tsar's performance as a leader during the war.

The war made people dislike the Tsar. Revolutionary groups were quick to feed this resentment. They argued that the war was not being fought in the interests of the people, but for the glorification of the Tsar and for the benefit of the wealthy manufacturers of weapons. Worst of all, the Tsar himself did not seem to care.

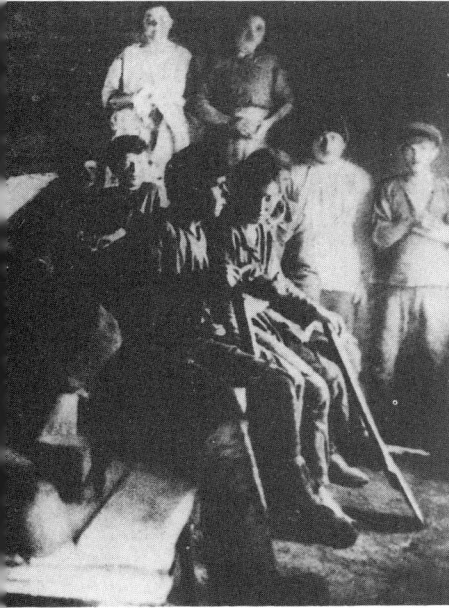

Tsarist troops ready to fire on demonstrators in January 1905.

1.2 FEBRUARY 1917: THE FIRST REVOLUTION

In February 1917 the tense situation in Russia became really explosive. Demonstrations broke out in Petrograd. ('St Petersburg' had been re-named because it sounded too German.) Women protesting about food shortages were supported by striking factory workers. Troops sent to stop the disturbances mutinied. They refused to fire on civilians and many joined the protests. This was not a planned revolution, but an uprising of people who could not bear any more hardship and oppression.

SOURCE B

'I greatly miss my half-hourly game of patience every evening. I shall take up dominoes in my spare time.'

Part of a letter sent by Nicholas II to his wife Alexandra on 8 March 1917, just as the revolution was beginning. Their children had measles and he could not see them.

SOURCE A

The soldiers joined the demonstrators. Here they are shown carrying banners with the slogan, 'Down with the monarchy', 10 March 1917.

The moderate reformers in the **Duma** (a sort of parliament with very limited powers) now had to decide how to respond to this movement. They could either lead the opposition to the Tsar, or be swept away by it. When moderates in the Duma tried to warn Nicholas of the danger of revolution he dismissed the Duma. Twelve members of the Duma ignored his instructions. On 16 March they demanded the Tsar's resignation, and set up a **Provisional Government**. Nicholas abdicated on behalf of himself and his son in favour of his brother, Grand Duke Michael. The next day Grand Duke Michael also abdicated, recognizing that hatred of rule by Tsars was so serious and widespread that the monarchy in Russia was doomed.

The Provisional Government included conservatives and liberals, and only one moderate socialist, **Kerensky**. It immediately declared that Russia was now a republic, and promised to hold elections for a new parliament as soon as possible. However, the Provisional Government had a more radical rival for power in the **Soviets**.

The popular protest in Petrograd was being led by the newly-created **Petrograd Soviet of Workers' and Soldiers' Deputies**. ('Soviet' is the Russian word for 'Council'.) Ordinary factory workers and soldiers chose representatives to go to the Soviet and defend their interests. Soviets soon sprang up in other industrial towns in Russia. Although they were not an official part of the government, the Soviets reflected closely the opinions of working people and soldiers. These were the very people who had made the revolution: the Provisional Government could not afford to ignore them.

At first the Provisional Government was popular. The revolution brought a mood of excitement and optimism. However, there were clearly problems ahead. Radicals exiled by the Tsar, and newly-released political prisoners, rushed to join in the protest and to help shape the future. They added to the Provisional Government's problems by demanding an end to the war and major reforms in land ownership and industry. The Provisional Government, which had developed from the conservative Duma, could not accept these demands.

SOURCE C

'That fat Rodzianko has sent me some nonsense. I shall not even reply.'

Nicholas II's response to a warning about the situation from a loyal member of the Duma, 12 March 1917.

SOURCE D

'The fact is that the revolution was begun from below, the initiative being taken of their own accord by the most oppressed and downtrodden part of the proletariat.'

Leon Trotsky, 'The History of the Russian Revolution', published in 1932.

SOURCE E

'The movement which has started has flared up without any party preparing for it and without any preliminary discussion of a plan of action. Now everything depends on the behaviour of the military units; if they do not join the working class, the movement will quickly subside; but if the troops turn against the government, then nothing can save the country from revolutionary upheaval.'

Part of a report by an Okhrana agent, 11 March 1917. (The Okhrana were the Tsar's political police.)

QUESTIONS

1 One historian wrote: 'Nicholas did not try to do anything to improve the situation. He did not even realize it was so bad.' Do you think that Sources B and C show that the Tsar did not care about the political problems in Russia?

2 How far, if at all, do Sources A and D support the statement that: 'This was not a planned revolution, but an uprising of people who could not bear any more hardship and oppression'?

1.3 THE SOLDIERS AND THE FEBRUARY REVOLUTION

EMPATHY

In 1905 the soldiers had played a vital part in the revolution because they had supported the Tsar. Some historians think that a crucial factor in the success of the 1917 Revolution was the change in the attitudes and actions of the soldiers.

Most Russian soldiers fighting in the First World War were peasants. Once the initial enthusiasm for the war had worn off, deep divisions between the officers and the soldiers were revealed. These divisions were matched by the dislike between classes that was obvious everywhere in Russia. Soldiers were not respected or admired for the sacrifices they were required to make. They were regarded as 'cannon fodder', as necessary losses in the effort to wear down the enemy. In the trenches the soldiers were ill-fed, poorly equipped and inadequately trained. The enormous numbers of casualties and deaths and the appalling conditions meant that many were increasingly reluctant to fight at all.

In February 1917 the soldiers in Petrograd were called on by the Tsar's ministers to deal with disturbances in the city. Most of these soldiers were new recruits, who were reluctant to go to the front.

SOURCE A

'General Ruzsky had complained to me of the lack of ammunition and the poor equipment of the men. There was a great shortage of boots. In the Carpathians the soldiers fought barefooted. The war hospitals were disorganized. They were short of bandages and such things.'

Rodzianko, President of the Duma, reporting to the High Commander of the Army in November 1914.

SOURCE B

Russian soldiers on the way to the Eastern Front carrying a banner which reads: 'On with the War for liberty', 1917.

EMPATHY

SOURCE C

'There is no more bread, nothing to eat. We sit here for days on end without bread. Cold and hunger, nothing but deprivation. I'd rather be killed than starve like a dog.'

An extract from a soldier's letter, confiscated by the censor in February 1917.

SOURCE D

'The work stoppage was total. Not a cab, not a doorman, not a bankclerk was on duty. Everyone poured onto the streets, possibly a majority of the city's population.'

Harrison E. Salisbury, a historian, on the people who took part in the February Revolution. From 'Russia in Revolution 1900–1930' , 1978.

SOURCE E

'Lenin said the only men who gained from the war were wealthy capitalist arms manufacturers. He urged the working classes not to fight and murder their proletarian brothers.'

E. M. Roberts, a historian, on Lenin's attitude to the war. From 'Lenin and the Downfall of Tsarist Russia', 1966.

They were ordered not to fire on the crowds listening to the public speeches. In fact the soldiers and even some Cossacks listened keenly to the debate. The first casualty of the revolution was a mounted police constable, shot by a Cossack soldier. The next day **Colonel Eksten**, commander of one of the Tsar's crack regiments, was killed by mutinous soldiers. The nature of the crisis had changed: street disorder had become a revolution.

On 27 February, at the meeting of the Petrograd Soviet in the Tauride Palace, soldiers' representatives arrived to declare the loyalty of their regiments to the cause of the people. As the name of each regiment was called out the hall rang with cheers.

SOURCE F

Russian soldiers deserting in early 1917.

EXERCISE

1 Sources A and C show that conditions at the front were terrible. We know that thousands of soldiers deserted during 1917. But Source B shows troops carrying a banner supporting the continuation of the war. Can you explain this contradiction?

2 Many of the soldiers taking part in the revolution came from rural areas, but most agricultural workers were not interested in political change. Can you explain this?

3 Source D lists the kinds of people, apart from the soldiers, involved in the street revolutions of February 1917. How is this relevant to historians trying to understand the behaviour of the soldiers?

1.4 THE PROVISIONAL GOVERNMENT

On pages 6-7 we saw how a series of unplanned riots turned into a major revolution. This revolt was tamed and changed by the middle-class liberals who came to power. Many business people and intellectuals felt that the revolution had gone far enough already by bringing about the downfall of the Tsar. They were now anxious to maintain control of the country by creating a **constitution** (or form of government) which guaranteed their rights and privileges. Their views were reflected in the attitude of the Provisional Government under **Prince Lvov** and Kerensky.

The Provisional Government had little real power. Its members had almost no practical experience of government. They had come to power in difficult circumstances, inheriting all the serious economic, social and political problems of the Tsar's regime. They argued that important decisions should not be taken until after the election of the new **representative assembly**. However, they did use their authority to liberalize Russia to a degree unknown before. Political prisoners were freed, and freedom of speech and of the press were allowed. In the long run this added to the problems of the government because their critics were able to make their complaints heard.

Most members of the Provisional Government wanted to change things gradually through consititutional reform. The majority of Russians, however, were concerned with more immediate problems. They wanted to know how the new government was going to respond to their demands for improvements in their living standards, changes in land ownership and an end to the war. Many working people and soldiers who were waiting for these changes grew impatient with the government. The promises made by more radical politicians began to look increasingly attractive.

The government decided that Russia should not pull out of the war, even though the war had been one of the major causes of the February Revolution. The government feared the Germans more than it feared the Soviets and radicals in Russia who were demanding peace. Moderates still believed that Russia could win the war, and felt obliged to Russia's allies on the Western Front. Kerensky, Minister of War from May and Prime Minister (in place of Lvov) from July 1917, also believed that a successful campaign against the central powers would win popularity for his government and help unite Russia.

SOURCE B

'We thought the revolution would bring peace. But now the counter-revolutionary Government forbids us even to talk of such things, and at the same time doesn't give us enough food to live on, or enough ammunition to fight with.'

A speech made at a public meeting in October 1917 by a soldier of the Forty-Sixth Siberian Army.

SOURCE A

'Citizens, the country still remains under the attack of a powerful enemy, who has seized whole provinces of our territory and now, in the days of the birth of Russian freedom, threatens us with new, decisive attacks. Defence at any cost to our own native land and liberation of the country from the enemy who has invaded its frontiers is the first duty of our soldiers, who are defending the liberty of the people.'

◀ *Part of a statement issued by the Provisional Government on 9 April 1917.*

A new offensive in the summer of 1917 failed. At the front the situation did not improve at all, and many more Russians were killed. Meanwhile the Bolsheviks recognized the strength of popular feeling against the war and encouraged it through constant anti-war **propaganda**. The Bolsheviks argued that the ordinary soldiers on both sides at the front should be allies rather than enemies. This appeal was very effective, and by July 1917 desertion from the army was commonplace.

Between February and October 1917 little progress was made on the question of land reform. Kerensky continued to argue that the problems should not be considered at all until after the elections. The government therefore concentrated on organizing the elections – a difficult task in a vast country with little experience of democracy. The peasants grew tired of waiting. Kerensky's government sounded increasingly like that of Tsar Nicholas, with constant demands for patience and hard work to help pull Russia through the immediate crisis.

In July 1917 there was another unplanned uprising in Petrograd. Soldiers, sailors and workers marched, shouting Bolshevik slogans and demanding the transfer of power to the Soviets. Four hundred people died in the disturbances. But the Provisional Government was not really in danger in July. Although the Bolsheviks were blamed for the troubles, they had not in fact encouraged the rioters, and they were not in a position to take power. Kerensky hoped that many Russians would prefer his government's moderate policies to the chaos that might follow a Bolshevik takeover. Many Bolsheviks, including Lenin, were forced into hiding and others were arrested. In the short term this was inconvenient for the Bolsheviks, but in the end it may have helped the reputation of their party. The Bolsheviks now appeared to be the only supporters of the revolution.

In August 1917 a right-wing general, **Kornilov**, led an attack against the radicals. He brought troops to Petrograd, aiming to hang all the political agitators there. Although Kerensky eventually joined the radicals in order to defeat Kornilov, at first he was suspected of supporting the general, and his government became even more unpopular. Kerensky's own authority and that of his government were slipping away. At last he promised to hold the elections to the Constituent Assembly in December. The announcement came too late: most Russians wanted immediate action over the war and land reform, and were not interested in waiting for constitutional reform. The Bolshevik opposition had been growing stronger. Soldiers had been deserting in enormous numbers and the peasants had begun to seize the land for themselves. The days of the Provisional Government under Kerensky were numbered.

SOURCE C

МЩЕНЬЕ ЦАРЯМЪ
(ВАРШАВЯНКА).

A Bolshevik poster condemning the war. It shows War, the Church and the Aristocracy riding on the shoulders of ordinary Russians.

QUESTIONS

1 What do you think were the main problems facing the Provisional Government in 1917? Which problems did members of the government think they should tackle at once? Which problems did they believe could be left for a while?

2 Is there any evidence in Source A to show that the Provisional Government had developed a war policy that differed in any way from that of the Tsar?

3 How did the Bolsheviks view the war?

4 With which view would working people and peasants have agreed?

1.5 THE OCTOBER REVOLUTION

In February 1917 most radical Russians, including many Bolsheviks, had welcomed the revolution as the first stage of Marx's predictions. They supported the Provisional Government. By the autumn the Bolsheviks, led by **Lenin** and **Trotsky**, were totally opposed to this same government. They now accused it of being counter-revolutionary. Why had this happened?

The turning point was Lenin's return from Switzerland in April 1917. In a speech to the Bolshevik Party, he made sweeping criticisms of the government and proposed a radical alternative programme. This became known as the **April Theses**. At first, even loyal party members dismissed the April Theses as being the response of a leader out of touch with the situation in Russia. The moderates in government did not believe that the Bolsheviks represented a threat.

Gradually the party saw that Lenin's view of the Provisional Government was right. In the meantime the government was preoccupied with the war effort and its preparations for the forthcoming elections. It failed to take any positive steps to deal with Russia's other urgent problems. Ordinary Russians were not benefiting from the revolution they had made. The war was still costing many lives, prices were rising and conditions all over the country were getting worse. Most people did not support the government which had failed to do anything about these serious difficulties. In contrast the Bolsheviks offered a popular alternative policy. Their plans for Russia came directly from the needs of the Russian people. They believed that power should belong to ordinary Russians.

Support for the Bolshevik Party grew rapidly. By June 1917 there were forty-one newspapers carrying Lenin's message across the country. The **'Red Guards'**, workers carrying rifles, were set up.

SOURCE A

Lenin, in 1918.

SOURCE B

Trotsky, in 1917.

SOURCE C

'The Kerensky government is against the people. He will destroy the country. This paper stands for the people and by the people – the poor classes, workers, soldiers and peasants. The people can only be saved by the completion of the Revolution, and for this purpose the full power must be in the hands of the Soviets. This paper wants:

- All power to the Soviets – both in the capital and in the provinces.
- Immediate truce on all fronts. An honest peace between peoples.
- Landlord estates, without compensation, to the peasants.
- Workers' control over industrial production.
- A faithfully elected Constituent Assembly.'

'Rabochi i Soldat', a pro-Bolshevik newspaper, October 1917.

By July there were 10,000 armed workers in Petrograd alone. Protesters adopted the Bolshevik slogan of 'All power to the Soviets!', even though the party's leaders knew they were not yet ready to seize power. In August the party had 200,000 members. By September the Bolsheviks dominated the Petrograd Soviet. Soon they controlled the Moscow Soviet too, and many other Soviets followed this example. Soldiers in Petrograd were dissatisfied with the government's war policy, and promised to help the party.

Why were the Bolsheviks, dismissed as idealistic dreamers early in 1917, so successful in throwing both the supporters of the monarch and the supporters of the Provisional Government into what Trotsky was to call 'the dust heap of history'?

In fact the 'party of dreamers' had leaders of exceptional quality. Lenin was an idealist who was prepared to risk his reputation and his life to turn his dreams into realities. He was a persuasive debater, winning the support first of his party and later of a majority of Russians. Trotsky shared many of Lenin's qualities, and was quickly won over by Lenin's view of the situation in 1917. He was also very practical – it was Trotsky's responsibility to organize the Red Guards during the October Revolution. Between them, Lenin and Trotsky provided leadership, organization and discipline. All members of the party respected their leaders and were dedicated supporters of the Bolshevik aims for Russia. This contrasted sharply with the position of the Provisional Government.

The Bolsheviks' policies were very popular with most Russians. During the so-called **Ten Days** of the October Revolution, more and more Russians opposed the Provisional Government. Kerensky's attempts to raise an army against the radicals failed because the soldiers were themselves the target of Bolshevik propaganda. They were also reluctant to attack their fellow Russians.

QUESTIONS

1 Make a copy of the time-line below. Use the map on page 22 to check that you know the whereabouts of all the places mentioned here.

2 Which incident or incidents do you think showed that the Provisional Government would not survive?

The October Revolution: ten days that shook the world

6 November	The Bolsheviks prepared for the uprising. They promised to give the people 'peace, land and bread' once the Soviets were in control. Lenin returned to the Bolshevik HQ in Petrograd.
7 November	Overnight the Red Guard took over key positions in Petrograd. Soldiers ordered to defend the Provisional Government's HQ deserted. By evening the Palace was under Bolshevik control. Many ministers were arrested. Kerensky fled to the front hoping to find loyal troops. The new government, called the **Council of People's Commissars**, was announced, with Lenin at its head.
8 November	The Soviets announced their programme. It was identical to that outlined in Source C. The Bolshevik uprising in Moscow was supported by 'government' troops. Ukrainian nationalists took Kiev, Mensheviks were in charge in Georgia. Kerensky's troops arrived in Petrograd but refused to act against their fellow Russians.
9 November	The Don Cossacks declared against the Bolsheviks. Kerensky still hoped to find a loyal

army under General Krasnov. A Bolshevik propaganda campaign began, designed to show that Kerensky was the enemy.

10 November	Krasnov's Cossack troops were closing on Petrograd. But the Cossacks did not strongly support the Provisional Government and prepared to return to the Don. The Provisional Government held the Kremlin in Moscow. The Bolsheviks in Saratov had siezed power but were threatened by the Cossacks.
11 November	The Bolsheviks in Petrograd appealed for support.
12 November	A truce was agreed in Moscow. The Red Guard in Petrograd defeated Krasnov's troops.
13 November	Sailors in Sevastopol forced their officers to take an oath supporting the Bolshevik government. The telephone exchange in Moscow was taken by the Red Guard.
14 November	The Cossacks outside Petrograd disbanded, believing that the Bolsheviks would not take their land.
15 November	Moscow was in the control of the Red Guard. Baku, centre of the oil industry, fell to the Bolsheviks.

1.6 WHY WAS THERE A SECOND REVOLUTION IN 1917?

CHANGE

Most people might have been able to predict that a revolution would happen in Russia. But when it took place in February 1917, it was unplanned. Few people expected another revolution in the near future. In October 1917 there was a second, planned revolution. What happened between February and October to convince the Bolsheviks that they could and should seize power?

SOURCE A

'From the wings the pale figure of the Minister made its way to the dais. He looked tired and ill. He drew himself up to his full height, as if calling up his last reserves of energy. As he finished he sank back into the arms of his aide-de-camp. In the limelight his face had the pallor of death. The whole audience cheered itself hoarse. It was an epic performance. The speech lasted 2 hours. Its effect on Russia lasted exactly 2 days.'

Bruce Lockhart on Kerensky in the summer of 1917.

SOURCE C

'Kerensky, a popular hero of the moment, was believed to be about to lead the Russian Revolution to the successful realization of its ideals, and was expected to bring land to the hungry peasants, land and peace to the weary soldiers without annexations or indemnities.'

Philips Price, an English journalist, later describing Kerensky as he had appeared in the summer of 1917.

SOURCE B

Lenin addressing a public meeting in the summer of 1917.

CHANGE

SOURCE D

Selected food prices, 1917 (in roubles)

	July	October
Lard (1lb)	1-10	5-40
Cheese (1lb)	1-60	5-40
Cabbage (1lb)	1-60	2-20
Sausages (1lb)	1-00	6-00

Bread rations, 1917 (per day)

	March	April	Sept.	Oct.
Manual workers	1½lbs	¾lb	½lb	¼lb
Others	1lb	¾lb	½lb	¼lb

Price increases and food shortages, February – October 1917.

SOURCE E

'Already desertion had set in wholesale. In very few cases did the men leave the front trenches, but as soon as they were moved they decamped in a body. Young students commanding thin extended lines of front could not possibly stop them. The root of the mischief was in Petrograd, and while the news which reached us continued to be very sinister, we were not able to understand what was really happening.'

An eyewitness account of the morale of the Russian soldiers at the front in April 1917.

SOURCE F

'Each year the peasants rented their land from the landowner. This year they went to him as usual and asked the usual rent. The peasants refused to pay it and without much bargaining went home. There they called a meeting and decided to take the land without paying. They got into an argument about the division of land, because it was not all the same quality. When they had quarrelled for some time, one of the party proposed that they proceed to the landowner's warehouse, where some good alcohol was kept. They broke into the place, where they found fifty barrels. They became so drunk that they carelessly set the place on fire. Four burned to death; ninety others escaped. A few days later they returned to the field and once more quarrelled. It ended with a fight in which thirteen were left dead, fifteen were carried off injured, and of these four died.'

The chaotic effect of revolutionary action without effective leadership in the countryside, as reported in a central newspaper in the summer of 1917.

SOURCE G

'The revolution is in danger! The people are in danger! We appeal to the people: Long live an immediate, honourable democratic peace, all power to the Soviets, all land to the people, long live the Constituent Assembly!'

Part of Trotsky's speech calling for support for the Bolshevik alternative programme in October 1917.

EXERCISE

1 Study the following list of causes of the October Revolution:
- Lenin's leadership of the Bolsheviks;
- the war;
- the peasants wanting to own their own land;
- food shortages in the towns;
- the failures of the Provisional Government;
- the policies of the Bolsheviks;
- the propaganda of the Bolsheviks.

For each cause, say:
a whether you think it was a **long-term** or a **short-term** cause;
b what you think the particular **effect** of this cause might have been.

In both cases explain the reasons for your answer.

2 Were all the causes listed in question 1 equally important? Give reasons for your answer.

3 Can the situation described in Source F be said to be a cause of the situation described in Source D? Explain your answer.

1.7 LENIN AND THE 1917 REVOLUTIONS

CAUSATION

Lenin played a vital role in the history of his country until his death in 1924. He is still respected and loved as the father of the USSR. (The **Union of Soviet Socialist Republics** was the name the Communist government gave to Russia in 1922.) In a country where hero worship is not usual, Lenin holds a unique position in the memory of its people and politicians.

In January 1917 Lenin gave a lecture in Switzerland on the twelfth anniversary of the 1905 Revolution. He did not believe there would be another revolution in his lifetime. Five days after the February Revolution began, he wrote to a friend in France to say that he had heard no news from Russia. Clearly Lenin, like all the other Bolshevik leaders, had not played a direct part in the February Revolution. Nevertheless, the Bolsheviks led an even more important revolution later that year. How important was Lenin's role in these events?

The Germans certainly believed that Lenin could cause trouble for the Russian government. They hoped that problems inside Russia would make the Russians less effective in the war. They helped Lenin return from exile, giving him safe passage through Germany in a 'sealed train'. He was not allowed to talk to anybody in case his ideas corrupted the German people.

Marx thought that one of the stages before socialism was a period of government by the middle classes. The Bolsheviks believed that the Provisional Government fulfilled this role. They expected a long period of development before there was any more change. But when Lenin got back in April 1917, he was not prepared to wait for long. He encouraged the Bolsheviks to think again and actively force through change.

Lenin made a stirring speech to his supporters when he arrived at the **Finland Station** in Petrograd. The next day he explained his reaction to the revolutionary events and outlined a new Bolshevik programme. He opposed the Provisional Government. He wanted the war to end. He wanted food for the workers and land for the peasants. These policies were completely different from those of Lenin's followers in Petrograd. Many Bolsheviks were surprised

SOURCE A

A summary of Lenin's 'April Theses'
1 Bolsheviks should oppose the war because it was fought for capitalist reasons.
2 Power should pass from the middle classes to the working classes.
3 Bolsheviks should not support the Provisional Government.
4 Soviets of Workers Deputies to form the basis of the new government.
5 The current police, army and bureaucracy to be abolished.
6 All landed estates to be confiscated.
7 A National Bank, controlled by a Soviet, was to replace all existing banks.

SOURCE B

'I shall never forget that thunderlike speech, startling and amazing not only to me, a heretic accidentally present there, but also to the faithful, all of them. Nobody expected anything of the kind. It seemed as if all the spirits of universal destruction had risen from their lairs to hover through the banquet chambers above the heads of the bewitched disciples.'

A non-Bolshevik response to the 'April Theses'.

SOURCE C

'A short, stocky figure, with a big head set down on his shoulders, bald and bulging. Little eyes, a snubbish nose, wide, generous mouth and heavy chin. Dressed in shabby clothes, his trousers much too long for him. Unimpressive, to be the idol of the mob, loved and revered as perhaps few leaders in history have been. A strange popular leader – a leader purely by virtue of intellect; colourless, humourless, uncompromising and detached, but with the power of explaining profound ideas in simple terms. His great mouth, seeming to smile, opened wide as he spoke; for emphasis he bent forward slightly. No gestures. And before him a thousand simple faces looking up in intent adoration.'

John Reed's description of Lenin, 8 November 1917. From 'Ten Days that Shook the World', 1926.

when Lenin adopted the slogan, 'All power to the Soviets!', believing he had made a serious political mistake. There were very few Bolshevik supporters in the Soviets at that time.

Lenin's radical ideas quickly found support among the workers in Petrograd. In July the Kronstadt sailors and some workers tried to push the party into an early **coup** (revolt) and demonstrated with banners supporting the Bolsheviks. Kerensky blamed the party for the disturbances and the bloodshed. Many Bolsheviks were arrested and others were forced into hiding or exile.

During the October Revolution, Lenin spent most of his time at the Bolshevik headquarters in Petrograd. Trotsky organized the details of the arrests and co-ordinated troop movements. Lenin formed a Bolshevik government and gave the 'People's Commissars' ministerial posts. On the day after the revolution he gave a speech demanding immediate peace negotiations and that all land should be owned by the state.

SOURCE D

A painting showing Lenin's arrival at the Finland Station, Petrograd in April 1917.

SOURCE E

◀ *A selection of stamps commemorating Lenin.*

EXERCISE

1 How would each of the following have reacted to reports about Lenin's speech in April 1917:

a a soldier at the front;
b a kulak (or wealthy peasant);
c a factory worker;
d a Bolshevik who had supported the Provisional Government;
e a German reporter?

Why do you think one man could have such a different effect on all these people?

2 Some of the things which happened in 1917 in the name of the Bolsheviks were beyond Lenin's control. Name one. Some events were influenced by Lenin. Describe one reason for the success of the October Revolution which was a result of Lenin's actions.

3 According to one historian, 'Lenin's arrival at the Finland Station in Petrograd was one of the decisive moments of the twentieth century.' Do you agree? Explain your answer.

2.1 THE BOLSHEVIKS IN CHARGE

The Bolshevik seizure of power in October 1917 was not seriously resisted at first. After only one week of fighting in Moscow and a few struggles elsewhere the Bolsheviks controlled most of Russia. Their main political rivals seemed unable to act. Lenin and the Bolsheviks knew that they had to work quickly to make sure their position was really safe.

The Bolsheviks had promised **'Peace, Land and Bread'** to the people of Russia. Now they faced the difficult realities of governing. Peace was achieved relatively easily in March 1918 by the **Treaty of Brest-Litovsk**, but at a huge cost to Russia. Russia lost one-third of its people, many of its railways and most of its coal mines and fertile agricultural land to Germany. Lenin recognized that the success of the Bolshevik revolution depended on meeting the people's demands, and on quickly gaining control of the country.

The long-awaited elections to the Constituent Assembly were allowed to go ahead. After the elections the Bolsheviks did not have a majority in the Assembly. They held about a quarter of the seats. As the Bolsheviks were still the government, they used their power to declare that the Assembly was not necessary. They argued that the people could be represented by the **Congress of Soviets**, where the Bolsheviks did have a majority. The Constituent Assembly was allowed to meet just once, in January 1918. Then it was dismissed by the Red Guard.

SOURCE B

'We are removing our armies and our people from the war. Our peasant soldiers must return to the land to cultivate in peace the fields which the revolution has taken from the landlord and given to the peasants. Our workmen soldiers must return to the workshops and produce not for destruction but for creation.'

Trotsky at the negotiations in Brest-Litovsk, 28 January 1918.

SOURCE A

Trotsky on the way to Brest-Litovsk to negotiate peace with Germany, 1918.

SOURCE C

'To the Citizens of Russia!
The Provisional Government
has been deposed. State power
has passed into the hands of
the Petrograd Soviet of
Workers' and Soldiers'
Deputies – the Revolutionary
Military Committee, which
leads the Petrograd proletariat
and the garrison.

The cause for which the
people have fought, namely, the
immediate offer of a democratic
peace, the abolition of landed
ownership, workers' control
over production and the
establishment of Soviet power –
this cause has been secured.

Long live the revolution of
workers, soldiers and peasants!'

*Poster written by Lenin announcing the
Bolshevik victory, 18 November 1917.*

SOURCE D

ТОВ. Ленин ОЧИЩАЕТ
землю от нечисти.

*This cartoon shows Lenin sweeping away
the old centres of power. The caption reads:
'Lenin cleans the earth of evil spirits'.*

Having abolished the Assembly, the Bolsheviks used their small majority in the Congress of Soviets to strengthen their control of Russia. The Congress's power was exercised through the **Presidium**. This was a committee dominated by the Bolsheviks, which allowed them to control central government. Local Soviets were also in the hands of the Bolsheviks. By mid-1918 the Presidium had declared that Russia was a **one-party state**, so there could be no official opposition to the Bolsheviks. Lenin argued that this was necessary in order to bring about the great changes to society which had been promised in the revolution. The Bolsheviks knew that they were dictators, but argued that they were acting in the interests of the proletariat. The Bolshevik Party was renamed the **Communist Party**. The party was all-powerful. Loyalty to the party was essential for anyone with ambition. Leadership of the party now carried with it huge power and responsibility.

In December 1917 the **Cheka** (the All-Russian Commission of Struggle against Counter Revolution, Speculation and Sabotage) was set up to deal with public order and crime. The Cheka quickly evolved into a formidable political police force. It dealt with all kinds of opposition to the government, enforcing the government's strict censorship laws and controlling all political activity. Its task was to defend the revolution from 'bourgeois' attacks. Sometimes innocent people suffered as the Cheka carried out its tasks. The Cheka acted very ruthlessly following an assassination attempt on Lenin in August 1918. In Petrograd alone over eight hundred so-called 'enemies of the people' were executed. This got rid of possibly dangerous opponents and set an example to others who might be considering opposition. The creation of the **Red Army** under Trotsky's leadership early in 1918 completed the party's means of control (see pages 24-5).

It seemed as if one dictatorship, that of the Tsars, had simply been replaced by another, that of Lenin and his Communist Party. A one-party state, a secret police and a 'party' army did not look like much of a change to most Russian citizens. The freedoms they had longed for, and had tasted, in 1917 seemed to have vanished as the new government tried to cope with the country's problems at home and abroad. The danger of a civil war was one excuse the Bolsheviks gave for their actions. Some argued that their actions made civil war even more likely.

CAUSATION

2.2 WHY WAS THERE A CIVIL WAR?

The Civil War was fought between the **Reds**, supporters of the Bolshevik revolution, and the **Whites**, a coalition of all those who opposed them. The Whites had the military, financial and moral support of almost the entire outside world. They were expected to defeat the Reds very quickly. But all that united the Whites was their desire to defeat the Reds. Each group in the coalition had different ideas about what was to follow their victory. This caused division in the White side, and helps to explain why they were unsuccessful.

Kerensky escaped during the Bolshevik coup of November 1917, and rushed to the front to raise troops to help defeat the revolutionaries in Petrograd. His supporters, **Kerenskyists**, wanted a return to the more limited revolution promised by the Provisional Government.

Members of the **Volunteer Army**, led first by Kornilov (the former Tsarist general who had led an unofficial attack on 'agitators' in August 1917) and later by **Denikin** (another former Tsarist), believed that they also represented the interests of the Provisional Government of February 1917. They thought that Russia's withdrawal from the First World War had been abrupt and unpatriotic, and they hated the 'shameful' Treaty of Brest-Litovsk. Most of the Volunteers were not fighting soldiers, who had welcomed the Bolshevik coup. Instead, they were former officers who found themselves at a loose end after the peace. The White Army was therefore 'top-heavy' – they had lots of officers but few experienced soldiers. The generals could not agree among themselves just who should lead. In November 1918 Denikin was appointed 'Dictator of Russia' by a joint Allied and White conference, and in December 1918 a White government at Omsk supported **Kolchak's** claim to be 'Supreme Ruler of Russia'.

The Russian bourgeoisie, particularly industrialists and former landowners, felt threatened by the Bolsheviks. They promised to support the Whites with money to fund their armies. In reality they provided little hard cash.

Kaledin, the ataman or leader of the **Don Cossacks**, claimed to represent the interests of all the Cossacks in his support of the Whites. In fact the majority of the Cossacks were not very interested in politics and believed that the Bolsheviks would redistribute the land in the Cossacks' favour anyway (see pages 26-7).

SOURCE B

'The Cossacks and the Bolsheviks are fighting savagely on the Don. A few days ago three sealed wagons with the inscription 'Fresh meat, destination Petrograd' arrived at one of the Petrograd stations. When the wagons were opened they were found to be filled with piles of the stiffened corpses of Red Guards, covered with frozen blood, with grimacing faces, placed in obscene positions. I certainly no longer have any sympathy for the Bolsheviks, but I cannot find words to describe this ghoulish farce.'

Louis de Bobien, French diplomat in Russia, 13 January 1918.

SOURCE C

'The workers of the towns and some of the villages choke in the throes of hunger. The railroads barely crawl. The houses are crumbling. The towns are full of refuse. Epidemics spread and death strikes to the right and to the left. Industry is ruined.'

Report in 'Pravda', 26 February 1920.

SOURCE A

'The rations were minute: black bread, a few herrings each month, a very small quantity of sugar for people in the 'first category' (workers and soldiers) and none at all for the 'third category' (non workers). Winter was torture – no heating, no lighting and the ravages of famine.'

Victor Serge, a dedicated revolutionary, on life in Petrograd during the Civil War. From 'Memoirs of a Revolutionary, 1901 – 41', 1963.

Lenin and many Bolsheviks feared that the former Tsar, Nicholas, provided a romantic rallying ground for the **Monarchists**. Lenin argued that the only alternative to Communism was a return to Tsarism. In fact the Monarchists were not strong or united, but the Bolsheviks were nervous of them. When the White Army threatened to take Ekterinburg, (the place where Nicholas and the royal family were being held) local Reds, apparently without official support, decided to kill the royal family. Very few Whites actually wanted a monarchy again, and few people in Russia were affected by these murders. Elsewhere in Europe the effect was more significant: refugees from the revolution helped to sway outside opinion against the Reds.

Russia's former allies, angered by the Bolshevik withdrawal from the First World War, refused to recognize the Treaty of Brest-Litovsk. They quickly rallied round the White opposition, which in turn promised to support the war effort against Germany. The Bolsheviks had proclaimed that their revolution would inspire a world-wide uprising, which caused great alarm in all capitalist countries. Anger over the war, and fears about the possible spread of Communism, were used to justify further interference in Soviet affairs by the so-called **Interventionists** long after Germany's collapse in 1918.

Between 1918 and 1921 the Bolsheviks had to deal with the armed forces of fourteen foreign powers, on six fronts. Britain alone committed £24 million to the struggle. The Interventionists had a profound effect on the Civil War. First, the money, weapons, food and trained men which they provided prolonged this bitter domestic conflict. Secondly, the Allies' interference helped to unite the Soviet people. They now saw themselves fighting a patriotic war in defence of Russia. The Whites were seen as traitors, not just as political opponents.

SOURCE D

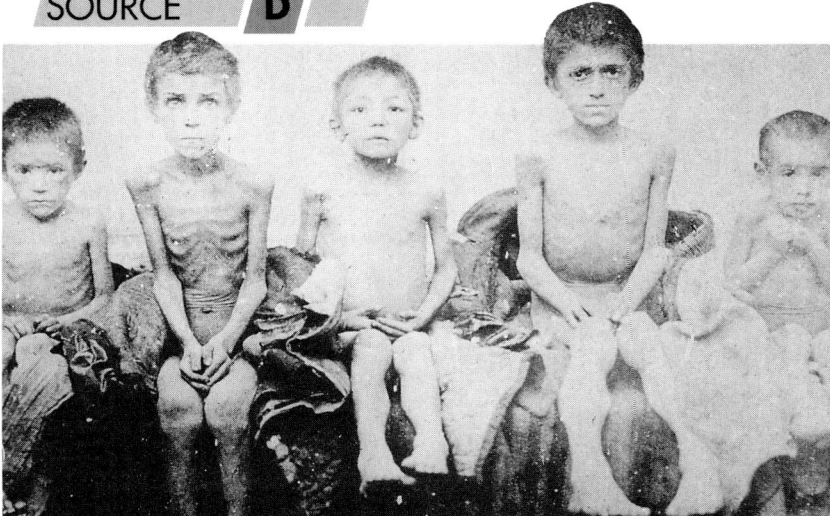

Starving children after the Civil War, 1921.

EXERCISE

1 a What do you think was the **motivation** of the Cossacks who loaded the train described in Source B?
  b What **effect** do you think the train might have had when it arrived in Petrograd? Give reasons for your answer.

2 a What **motives** made people support the Reds?
  b What **motives** made people support the Whites?
  c Do you think the difference between your answers to parts **a** and **b** means that either the Reds or the Whites had an advantage over the other? Explain your answer.

3 In 1917 the Bolsheviks promised 'Peace, Land and Bread'. However, the country was involved in a bloody civil war and there was such a food crisis that people died from starvation.
  Does this mean:
  • the Bolsheviks were lying;
  • in History what people want does not affect what happens;
  • the Bolsheviks said what they wanted to happen, but something else happened anyway?

Which one do you think is the best answer?
Explain your reasons.

2.3 THE CIVIL WAR, 1918-20

The end of the First World War was welcomed by most Russians –
but it was followed by a very serious and vicious civil war. The new
government was attacked by many different groups within Russia.
They were also attacked from outside by the Western Allies, who
supported the Whites. The Allies believed that the defeat of the Reds
would bring Russia back into the war against Germany.

SOURCE A

'Each drop of Lenin's blood
must be paid for by the
bourgeoisie and the Whites in
hundreds of deaths. It is time
for us to be pitiless.'

*From a Petrograd newspaper, following an
attempt on Lenin's life in 1920.*

SOURCE B

'The workers in the towns and
some of the villages choke in
the throes of hunger. The
railroads barely crawl. The
houses are crumbling. The
towns are full of refuse.
Epidemics spread and death
strikes to the right and to the
left. Industry is ruined.'

Report in 'Pravda', 26 February 1920.

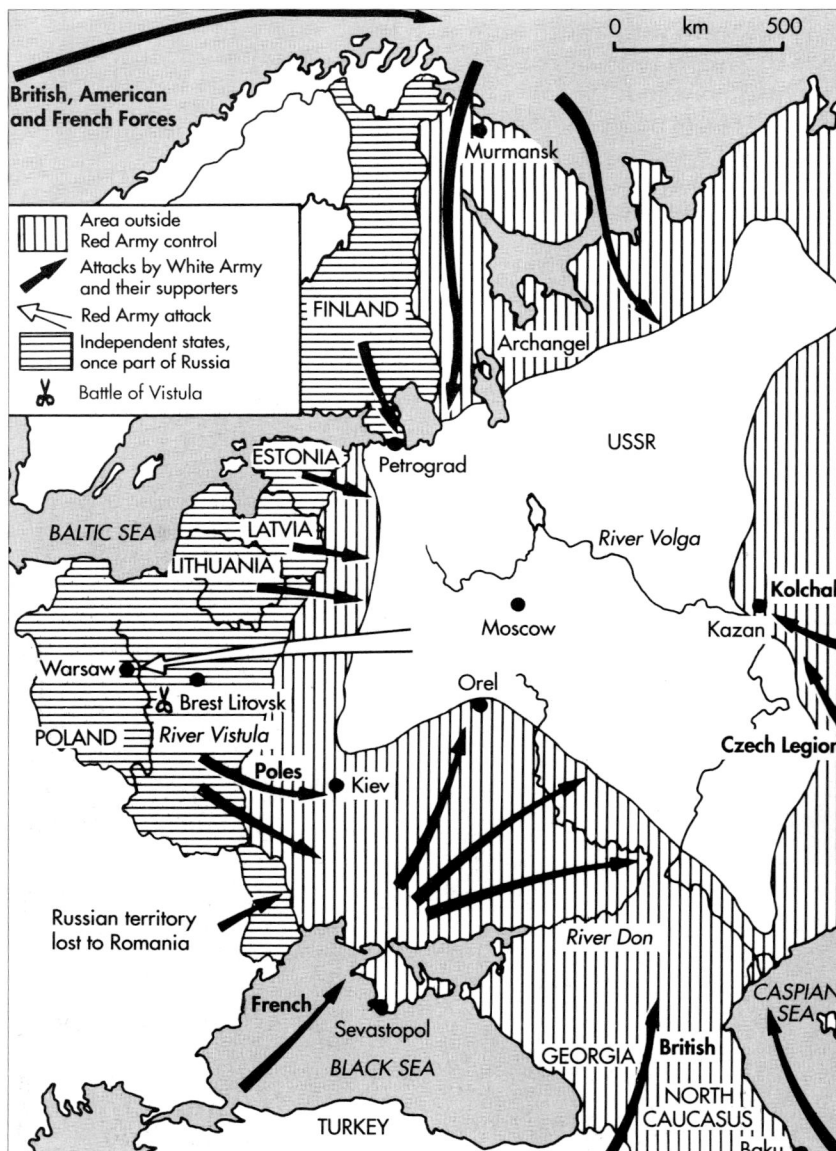

Bolshevik territory during the Civil War.

SOURCE C

*A Bolshevik cartoon, 1920. The caption
reads: 'A Red present for the White
noblemen'.*

The Red Army was vulnerable – but was united under Trotsky's inspired leadership. The Reds also controlled the heartland of the country, and with it all the internal lines of communication (see map). Most ordinary Russians believed that the Reds represented their interests in defending the revolution. In particular, the Bolshevik land settlement was very popular. The Whites, on the other hand, were not united. They represented a mixture of very different groups who did not work effectively together. Most Russians thought the Whites were unpatriotic because they were receiving help from foreign powers hostile to the government of Russia.

The Civil War lasted two years. Terrible atrocities were committed on each side, including the massacre of the Tsar and his family. An attempt on Lenin's life in August 1918 encouraged Bolshevik supporters to call for severe punishments against White supporters.

The long-term consequences of the Civil War were serious too. Russia had already suffered years of bad government under the Tsar. The First World War had disrupted the economic life of the countryside and towns. Now starvation threatened the whole country. Nevertheless, most Russian peasants and the working classes in the towns were delighted by the triumph of the Reds.

QUESTIONS

1 What advantages did the Red Army have during the Civil War?

2 What disadvantages did the Whites have?

3 Why did most Russians support the Bolsheviks despite the continuing hardships they faced between 1918 and 1920?

4 What new problems do the sources suggest the Bolshevik government would have to face at the end of the Civil War?

SOURCE D

A group of starving peasants, 1921.

2.4 TROTSKY AND THE RED ARMY

CAUSATION

Trotsky was surprised by the February Revolution. He had been living and working in exile in New York. He tried to return to Russia, but was held up by the British, who put him in a concentration camp in Nova Scotia. He finally got to Petrograd in May 1917. In the past Lenin and Trotsky had argued over how to interpret Marx's work. Faced with the reality of the revolution, Trotsky was quickly swayed by Lenin's views. Within six weeks he was clearly regarded by Lenin as his 'number two' in the Bolshevik Party. Other Bolsheviks accepted Trotsky, but always saw him as a rival. Trotsky played a major part in organizing the October Revolution that brought the Bolsheviks to power.

Even before the end of 1917, Kornilov and other hostile generals began to organize the White opposition to the Communists. As the opposition against the new regime grew, it seemed as if Lenin's government was in a very dangerous position. The Bolsheviks had been partly responsible for the collapse of the army. Their propaganda had led to mass desertions. They had also demanded other reforms like the abolition of the death penalty in the army and the introduction of elections for officers.

In March 1918 Trotsky resigned as Commissar for Foreign Affairs and became **Commissar for War** and **Chairman of the Supreme War Council**. Lenin made it clear that he considered Trotsky the only person able to save the revolution, saying: 'Who else can we appoint? Name them.' Trotsky did lead the Red Army brilliantly, and the Red Army saved the revolution.

SOURCE B

Trotsky addressing his troops from the top of an armoured car.

SOURCE A

SOURCE C

'I felt like a surgeon who has finished a difficult and dangerous operation – I must wash my hands, take off my apron and rest. Lenin was in a different position. He had just arrived from his refuge, after spending three and a half months cut off from real, practical direction.'

Trotsky's account of his position at the end of November 1917, in 'My Life', published in 1930.

◀ *Lenin and Trotsky were close political allies during the revolution and the Civil War.*

CAUSATION

Trotsky in front of his specially equipped train.

SOURCE **E**

'Gomel was just about to fall into the enemy's hands when Trotsky arrived. Then everything changed and the tide began to turn. Trotsky's arrival meant that the city would not be abandoned. Trotsky paid a visit to the front lines. He made a speech. We were lifted by the energy which he carried wherever a critical situation arose. The situation, catastrophic but 24 hours earlier, had improved by his coming as though by a miracle.'

Alexander Barmine's description of the effect of Trotsky's leadership.

Trotsky recognized the importance of personal contact with his troops. He toured Russia constantly during the Civil War, bringing hope and courage to his troops. He travelled in a special train which had everything he needed for the conduct of the war. It was a mobile office and home which also carried crack troops, extra weapons and ammunition, medical supplies, boots, tobacco and propaganda. He was able to take help quickly to wherever it was needed most, calling on reinforcements if necessary.

The Red Army was run on traditional lines. Trotsky did not carry out any of the reforms that he had previously wanted for the army. He argued that the Civil War was not a time for experiments. Trotsky took a practical approach. He appointed former army officers who were willing to serve in the Red Army, because their skills were vital. He resorted to conscription because a larger army (of some 5 million at the height of the war) was needed to defeat the Whites. Trotsky also recognized that the morale and loyalty of the army was as essential as its skills and size. The core of the army always consisted of dedicated volunteers. The appointment of party members at every level encouraged devotion to the cause. Commissars now shared authority with officers. One was responsible for the morale and loyalty of the troops, the other for military training. Harsh discipline was used to make sure the troops stayed loyal. Above all, Trotsky's fairness made the Red Army different from the old Imperial army. Trotsky was loved and respected by his men, and together they saved the revolution: the Whites were defeated. Also, the foundations were laid for the large, dedicated and patriotic force that was to stand up to the Nazi attack during the Second World War (see pages 58-9).

In the long term, Trotsky may have been a victim of his own success. While he was busy managing the war, other party members gave themselves important jobs within the party. Once the war was over, Trotsky found himself a hero without a role. He was outside the circle of powerful party members like Stalin. Some even suggested that Trotsky was prepared to use the Red Army against the state to further his own ambitions.

EXERCISE

1 Why do you think the British government did not want Trotsky to return to Russia in 1917?

2 In what ways might Trotsky's practical abilities and successes have helped later to exclude him from power?

3 The Red Army would have existed without Trotsky's leadership, but its success is often attributed to Trotsky. List any of Trotsky's policies in relation to the organization of the army which were his special contribution.

2.5 THE COSSACKS, 1906-18

EMPATHY

Tsar Nicholas II in Cossack uniform with a company of Cossack officers.

The **Cossacks** of the Russian prairies have been famous for centuries for their courage and debauchery. They have been both feared and admired. The part they have played in Russian history has varied too. Sometimes they were seen as the champions of the weak in society, encouraging peasant revolts by resisting authority. At other times they were seen as ruthless oppressors. By the late nineteenth century the Cossacks were under the Tsar's control and provided an elite cavalry force in his army. The Cossack soldiers were seen as the Tsar's chief henchmen. Twentieth-century radicals could not forget their role in crushing the 1905 Revolution.

Between 1906 and 1918 the Cossacks changed sides with amazing speed. At the beginning of the First World War the Cossacks were enthusiastic supporters of the Tsar. Cossack farmers rushed to enlist. In the past the mounted Cossacks had been a formidable fighting force. Trench warfare, with barbed wire, machine guns, lorries and even aircraft, reduced the need for a cavalry. The British and French cavalry were quickly withdrawn from the battlefield, but the Cossacks were still used, despite the unsuitable conditions. This led to great resentment against the Tsar. The Cossacks who were left at home also faced enormous difficulties. No new farm machinery was available at a time when the labour force was drastically reduced. Livestock was slaughtered and grain supplies diminished.

By 1917 it was clear that the Cossacks were angered by their wartime experiences. Even so, when the revolution began in Petrograd nobody really knew how the Cossack troops would behave. The crowds were delighted when the Cossacks joined the revolution.

At first the Cossacks were staunch defenders of the Provisional Government. By the late summer their loyalties were changing. They did not help Kornilov in his attempt to crush the Bolsheviks.

'The Cossacks, notwithstanding a number of orders, have not come out of their barracks up to this time. The Provisional Government is in danger of losing all its power.'

Telegram from Colonel Plokovnilov in Petrograd to General Dukhonin, Commander-in-Chief at the front, 24 October 1917.

'You Cossacks are being incited to act against us workers and soldiers. This plan of Cain is being put into operation by our common enemies, the oppressors, the privileged classes – generals, bankers, landlords, former officials, former servants of the Tsar.'

From a Bolshevik pamphlet given to Cossacks guarding the Winter Palace, 25 October 1917.

'The Cossack government declares that it considers the acts of the Bolsheviks criminal and inadmissible. Until the return of the Provisional Government to power and the restoration of order in Russia, I have taken on myself all power in that which concerns the region of the Don.'

Ataman Kaledin, leader of the Don Cossacks.

EMPATHY

Cossacks in Petrograd did nothing to stop the Bolshevik coup of October 1917. Many Cossacks now returned to their homelands, hoping to forget the war and the revolution. They wanted to be left in peace to cultivate their lands in the traditional way.

But it was soon clear that the Bolshevik revolution in Petrograd would affect the Cossacks more seriously than they had expected. The Red Army moved into the Cossack homelands, siezing supplies and threatening Cossack society by talking about equality. Within months the Don Cossacks were providing shelter for the White generals who wanted to defeat the revolution. By May 1918 the Red Army had been forced from the Don region. During the Civil War most of the White Army's volunteer troops came from Cossack groups. What motivated the Cossacks?

EXERCISE

1 Many Cossacks came from poor peasant families. Why did they support the Tsar's regime at first against the protests of other poor people?

2 Study Sources A and E. Do you think the Cossacks pictured with the Tsar would have a different attitude towards him than those referred to in Source B? Explain your answer.

3 The Cossacks had been among the Tsar's most loyal supporters, yet in February 1917 they did nothing to save his government. Does this mean they had changed their ideas?

4 The Cossacks had a reputation for bravery and ferocity. In October 1917 they would not leave their barracks to defend the Provisional Government. Does this mean they were cowards?

SOURCE **E**

A Cossack charge against the Germans during the First World War.

2.6 COMMUNIST PROBLEMS IN GOVERNMENT, 1917–21

Lenin's Communist government had to face difficult economic, social and political problems. These problems had already brought about the downfall of the Tsarist state and of the Provisional Government. The Tsars had ignored them. The Provisional Government had not recognized the need for urgent action. The Communists were ready to tackle them. They believed that far-reaching changes were needed in order to take advantage of the 1917 revolutions and to defend the new Communist state.

Lenin was determined to deal with these problems. 'We will now proceed to construct the Socialist order', he stated. Some of the measures taken during this period were harsh, and the methods of the government were dictatorial. The Bolsheviks called this period **'War Communism'**. Special measures were needed to deal with a national emergency.

The Communists recognized that Russia's economic and social problems were closely related. One of the government's first measures was intended to solve both problems. The **Supreme Council of National Economy** was set up to organize a planned economy and so create a fairer society. The economy would be organized around communal interests (the interests of everybody), rather than self-interest (the interests of individuals). By mid-1918 War Communism in fact meant that the government controlled all economic activity. Citizens were now expected to regard each other as brothers, and all profit was considered exploitation. However, Bolshevik ideas of 'community' and 'equal shares' meant little to ordinary people. During the war there was no time for persuasion. The government had to force these important changes in ideas on to a reluctant workforce. The peasants who had supported the Bolsheviks in 1917 had done so because they wanted to own the land they worked on and paid rent for. They wanted to profit from their own work. They wanted to join the kulak or rich peasant class, not to replace it. Many peasants resented the government's attempts to force Communist ideals on them.

As the Civil War got worse, the government controlled the work-force. Peasants were 'regimented' and their crops were taken. Officials encouraged the peasants to work harder still, and unco-operative peasants were disciplined. Many bitterly resented this extra pressure. By 1921 the economy was again at breaking point. There was not enough food for the towns and some peasants began to hide any surpluses for their own benefit. More people died of hunger during the Civil War than from the fighting. Despite very harsh government action against the peasants, food production continued to fall. The Bolsheviks were failing to deliver one important promise to the people of Russia – there was still not enough 'Bread'. War Communism was not working.

In March 1921 the Kronstadt sailors revolted against the government, calling for 'Soviets without Communism'. The sailors had been loyal supporters of the Bolsheviks, but they now felt betrayed by them. They thought War Communism did not reflect any of the original aims of the rebels of 1917. **'Red Kronstadt'** was brutally put down by the government. Several thousand rebels were killed or wounded, or went missing.

SOURCE A

1 Political freedom for all socialist parties.
2 Free elections to the Soviets.
3 An immediate end to grain requisitions.
4 Free trade to be established.

List of the Kronstadt sailors' demands.

SOURCE **B**

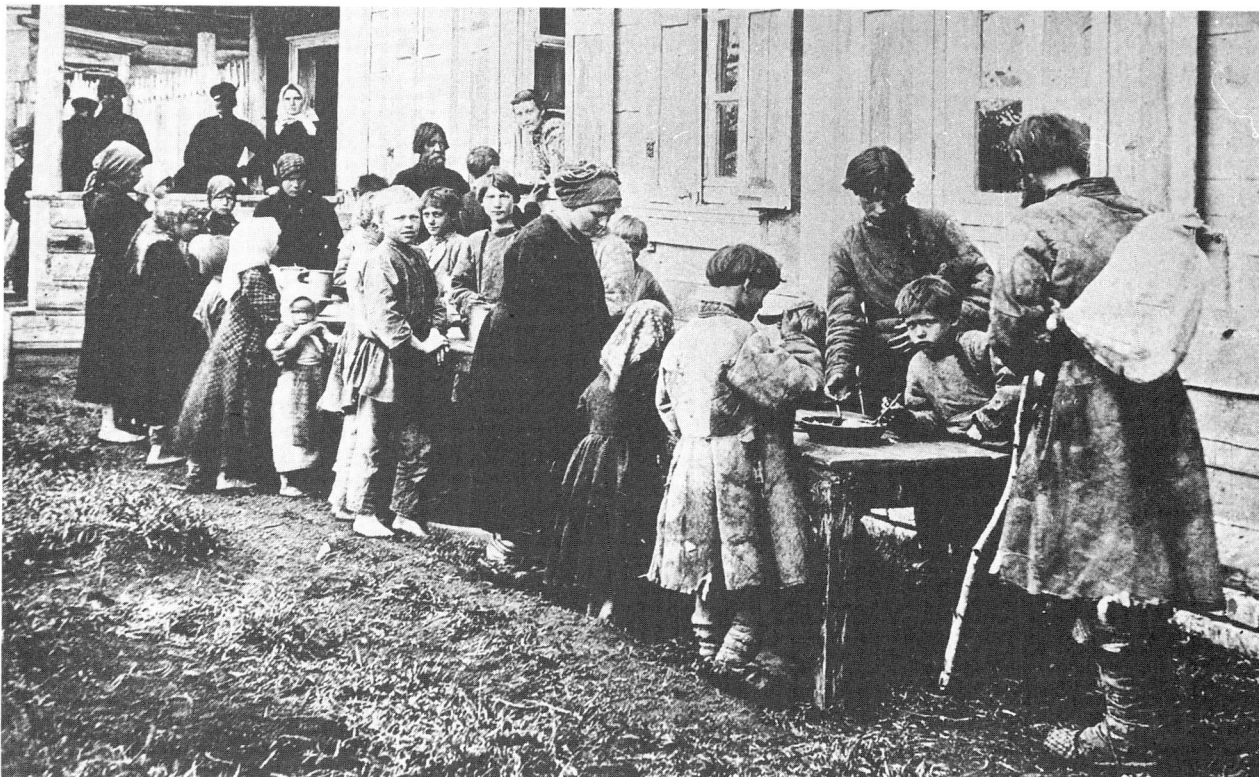

A meal being organized for some poor villagers in about 1921.

Lenin and Trotsky knew that, unless Communism was modified, the Communist state was doomed. War Communism had been essential for the revolution to survive the challenge by the Whites. Something less harsh was now essential if Communism was to survive at home. Lenin was a practical politician, and he began to prepare a new economic policy more suited to the needs of 1921. He wanted to win back the support of the peasants, the armed forces and the industrial workers – the proletariat that the revolution had been intended to serve.

QUESTIONS

1 Before 1917 Lenin and the other Communist leaders had been against the Tsar's government because it was harsh and repressed people. How could they justify War Communism?

2 **a** Look at Source A. Had the Communist government failed to fulfil its revolutionary promise?

   b Why was this?

3 Why did the Communist government suppress the Kronstadt uprising of 1921?

3.1 NEW POLICIES AND NEW LEADERSHIP, 1921-24

The New Economic Policy

In 1921 Lenin abandoned War Communism and introduced the **New Economic Policy** (NEP). This was a response to the grave problems we have seen on pages 28-9. He recognized now that the ideal of Communism could not be achieved at once. People of all classes had to be educated to see the benefits Communism could offer. The NEP created a **mixed economy**, where Communism and capitalism would develop side by side. Lenin desperately needed to get the economy moving again after the disruption of the Civil War. Lenin also realized that he had to have the support of the peasants when he said: 'Only agreement with the peasants can save the socialist revolution in Russia.' He was a practical revolutionary, willing to adopt any policy to save the revolution. To more eager revolutionaries this looked like a step backwards which would delay the fulfilment of Bolshevik dreams.

In May 1922 the **Fundamental Law** was passed in the USSR. This gave the peasants more rights in land ownership and more freedom to sell or lease their land. They were allowed to use hired labour and sell any surplus food they produced for profit. Small industries could be privately owned, but heavy industries, foreign trade, the transport system and major banks remained under strict government control. The NEP only went a small way towards restoring capitalism, but by 1925 it had begun to work. The rural community provided enough food to keep the workers in the towns fed. In this way, economic stability was restored in the USSR, although it was not until 1926 that production had reached even 1913 levels. The wider economic freedom allowed after 1922 was not matched by any greater political freedom. Opponents were still being rounded up and imprisoned or sent to Siberia.

Lenin's death

Lenin died in 1924. In his last years he had been worried by the problems of moving from partial Communism to full Communism, and by the question of who should succeed him as party leader. The real choice was between **Trotsky** and **Stalin**, both of whom had given good service during the revolution. Other contenders were **Kamenev** and **Zinoviev**, the leaders of the Communist Party in Moscow and Petrograd. They had been Lenin's loyal supporters from the earliest days of the revolution.

Lenin probably favoured Trotsky, although he did have doubts about Trotsky's political judgement. He was also worried by Trotsky's enthusiasm for the idea of a revolution throughout the world. Trotsky's power base was the Red Army. He did not have much support among the old party, who had always been suspicious of him. Kamenev and Zinoviev were not pleased when Lenin appeared to favour Trotsky as a successor. They disliked both his policies and his manners. They proved to be dangerous enemies of Trotsky. Their alliance with Stalin following Lenin's death kept Trotsky out of power. Lenin was not convinced that Stalin was the right man to lead the party. Lenin and Stalin did not get on well personally, even though Stalin looked after Lenin during his last illness.

SOURCE A

The restoration of street trading following the NEP. A street market in Smolensk, 1921.

SOURCE B

'We hoped to found state industries and organize distribution on a Communist basis in a country that was petit-bourgeois. Life has shown that we made a mistake. A succession of transition periods was required to prepare, through many years of preliminary work, the transition to Communism.'

Lenin's speech to the Communist Party Conference in 1921.

SOURCE C

'I am sure that Trotsky will be able to stand up for my views just as well as I myself.'

Lenin on Trotsky, 15 December 1922.

Stalin's power base was the Communist Party itself. He had become General Secretary, which meant he could decide who got the important jobs in the party. In this way he had been able to build up loyal support. In the end Stalin's greater personal ambition and his political skills triumphed. While Lenin was ill Stalin carefully created a public impression of closeness between himself and the leader of the Bolsheviks.

When Lenin died in 1924 Trotsky was ill, leaving Stalin to make all the funeral arrangements. Stalin was seen by thousands of other mourners standing at the coffin, and he gave the funeral oration. In praising the dead leader he began a process of public worship of Lenin. As a chief mourner, Stalin appeared the rightful heir to Lenin's power.

By 1928 Stalin was completely in charge in the Soviet Union. He had blocked Trotsky's progress in the party with the help of Zinoviev, Kamenev and a group of loyal supporters. Zinoviev and Kamenev were worried by Stalin's misuse of power within the party, but were unable to stop him. They even attempted to form an alliance with Trotsky, but failed to have any effect. Stalin took control of their power bases in Moscow and Leningrad (the new name for Petrograd) in 1926. In 1927 Trotsky was expelled from the Communist Party. Zinoviev and Kamenev were disgraced in the same year. Nothing and nobody could stop Stalin from taking the Soviet Union on whatever path he chose.

SOURCE   D

'With best comradely greetings, Lenin.'

The end of Lenin's last letter to Trotsky.

SOURCE   F

Stalin at Lenin's coffin in 1924.

SOURCE   E

'I ask you whether you are prepared to withdraw what you have said and to make your apologies, or whether you prefer that relations between us should be broken off. Respectfully yours, Lenin.'

A letter from Lenin to Stalin after a domestic quarrel between Stalin and Lenin's wife, 5 March 1923.

3.2 STALIN, IMAGE MAKER

EVIDENCE

Stalin was well aware of the importance of his **image**. The impression he made on the party, on ordinary Soviet people and on the rest of the world all affected the way in which he could govern. He was careful to develop an image which added to his authority. He stressed qualities which he believed would make people respect him, and hid those which might have damaged his reputation.

In this unit you will look at the impression that Stalin wanted to make, the effect of his control of the media and the consequences of this, both for the people around him and for historians.

SOURCE B

Lenin and Stalin in Gorky, 1922.

SOURCE A

'Comrade Stalin, having become General Secretary, has concentrated immeasurable power in his hands, and I am not sure he knows how to use that power with sufficient caution. Stalin is too rude, and this fault, though tolerable in dealings among us Communists, becomes unbearable in a General Secretary. Therefore I propose to the Comrades to find some way of removing Stalin from his position and appointing somebody else who differs in all respects from Comrade Stalin.'

An analysis of Stalin's qualities taken from Lenin's 'Testament', 4 January 1923.

SOURCE C

Stalin being hugged by a child during May Day celebrations, 1952.

EVIDENCE

SOURCE D

Lenin and Stalin in Gorky. This statue was commissioned in 1939 when Stalin was in supreme power. Copies were seen all over Russia.

SOURCE E

Part of a May Day celebration in 1952.

EXERCISE

1 What does Source B tell us about the relationship between Lenin and Stalin shortly before Lenin's death?

2 How does Source D support Source B?

3 Does this mean that Sources B and D are reliable?

4 Does Source A support the impression given by Sources B and D?

5 Which of Sources A, B and D do you think is the most useful for assessing the true nature of Lenin's relationship with Stalin?

6 Which of Sources A, B and D do you think had most impact on Soviet citizens after Lenin's death in 1924?

7 We know that Stalin was a capable and ruthless politician. What impression was he trying to create in Sources C and E?

8 Who do you think he was trying to impress with this image?

9 Would Stalin want everyone in the Soviet Union to see him in this way? Can you think of any groups which Stalin would want to affect in a different way?

10 Does Source E prove that Stalin was successful in persuading the Soviet people that he was a good leader?

3.3 PEASANT RESISTANCE TO CHANGE

CHANGE

The peasants put up great resistance to any reforms in agriculture. Their attitudes made it difficult for the government to create the Communist state it had promised. When the Bolsheviks gave the land to the peasants after the October Revolution, the peasants were satisfied. They now wanted to be left in peace to farm their land. They did not see the link between industrial and agricultural development in the Soviet Union, and did not care about the industrial workers. The Bolshevik Party always hoped that the peasants would work together for the common good. This simple notion was not understood by most peasants.

During the Civil War, famine threatened the towns. The government controlled the sale of all food to make sure the workers in the towns got fed. The peasants were angry at the government's action, and the emergency measure backfired. The peasants simply refused to grow any more food than they needed for themselves. They could not see any point in working hard without gaining anything for themselves. Much less food was produced and many people starved as a result.

After the Civil War, Lenin knew that the economy needed to be encouraged. The peasants had to have incentives if they were to produce enough to feed themselves and the growing towns. At this time most of the party was convinced by Lenin's argument that 'only agreement with the peasants can save the socialist revolution in Russia'. The NEP encouraged private enterprise, particularly in the countryside. The Fundamental Law of May 1922 guaranteed the peasants' rights to the land, and allowed them to sell or lease their land freely and to hire labour. Some party members saw the NEP as a return to the system they had overthrown.

SOURCE B

Harvesters in 1923 using long-handled scythes.

SOURCE C

'A dozen or so open-faced boys took us out to show us the tractors. I remember the enthusiasm of one of them. "Come on, and fix this one first," he told us, dragging us over to the corner of a ragged-looking wheat field where a tractor listed hopelessly. "Very good tractor," he said, pointing to a hole in the top of the radiator beside the radiator cap, "marvellous for boiling potatoes." Of the twelve tractors only three were working. The rest were in various stages of disintegration.'

J. Scott, an American engineer, in his book 'Behind the Urals', 1942.

SOURCE A

◀ *Peasants examining the first tractor to arrive in their village in 1926.*

SOURCE D

Four peasants on a collective farm in the 1930s, attending an adult literacy class.

Plans for a system of agriculture based on collective ownership had to be shelved for the time-being (see pages 38-9). The peasants continued to work on their small farms, using old-fashioned and unproductive farming methods. The government still hoped to persuade a majority of peasants that there were advantages for both the countryside and the towns in greater co-operation. The peasants preferred their traditional farming methods and way of life. The government grew impatient with the peasants' failure to adopt Communism. Some peasants were accused of being 'wreckers' – trying to defeat Communism through a combination of deliberate sabotage and simple lack of enthusiasm.

EXERCISE

1 How did peasant attitudes towards the Bolshevik government change between 1917 and 1925?

2 How did the Bolshevik government's attitude towards the peasants change between 1917 and 1925?

3 When and why did production levels fall between 1917 and 1925?

4 Source C illustrates some of the problems the government faced in trying to modernize farming. Does it help us to understand why and how peasant attitudes needed to change if collectivization was ever going to succeed?

5 Tractors make farming easier and help farmers get better crops. Does this mean that peasants would approve of changes in the countryside which meant there were more tractors?

6 Despite government propaganda, good-quality farm machinery was not widely available during this period. How would this affect peasant attitudes towards collective farming?

3.4 **SOCIALISM IN ONE COUNTRY**

By 1923 it was clear that Communism had not spread throughout Europe as the Bolsheviks had predicted in 1917. The Communist Party was now forced to accept that it was surrounded by completely hostile neighbours. Foreign governments were anxious to protect themselves from all Communist influence. This meant that the Communist Party had to think again about its policy of spreading revolution.

Stalin's policy was developed from a variety of sources. From Trotsky he took the idea that rapid **industrialization** was the key to the USSR's survival. From Trotsky's enemies he took the idea that socialism could, after all, be developed 'in one country'. He saw that he could not wait for a world revolution to solve the USSR's political problems. He decided to concentrate only on the needs of the USSR itself. This combination of ideas was to prove more successful, and was followed ruthlessly through the **collectivization of agriculture** (see pages 38-9) and the **Five-Year Plans** for the development of industry. Stalin had skilfully chosen policies which would suit the needs of the USSR. He had also combined them in a way which left him firmly in control.

The policy of **socialism in one country** was developed against a background of clever political manoeuvring during which Stalin made himself undisputed leader of the USSR. Trotsky and other potential rivals and critics were discredited, exiled and eventually killed. The impressive, if intensely suspicious, figure of Stalin was to dominate and shape Soviet political life for more than a generation.

The longer Stalin stayed in power, the more anxious he became about his own role in history. He was not content simply to eliminate his rivals and opponents – he had to eradicate them from history too.
Source A is a photograph of Stalin and his colleagues taken in April 1925.
Source B was published, after retouching, twenty four years later. The photographs show the same scene, but five of Stalin's former colleagues have been erased.

SOURCE A

QUESTIONS

1 Compare the two photographs in Sources A and B. If you had only seen Source B would you have guessed that it was a reconstruction?. Explain your answer.

2 Source B is not a very good forgery. Why do you think Stalin and his publicists believed Soviet citizens would be fooled by it?

SOURCE **B**

3.5 THE COLLECTIVIZATION OF AGRICULTURE

In 1928 famine threatened the Soviet Union again. The towns could not be fed on the amount of food supplied by the country's 25 million peasant landowners and handful of state farms. Agricultural and industrial development were very closely connected. Stalin knew that industrialization was vital if the Soviet Union was to compete with the hostile industrial powers. If agriculture could be made more efficient, it could feed the industrial workers and perhaps even provide a surplus of grain to export. This would raise foreign money for investment in industry. Larger farms would also need to be **mechanized**. This would create a new market for farming equipment which would in turn stimulate many related industries. It is easy to see why Soviet economists were so keen to modernize agriculture. The huge obstacle to such reform was the peasant farmers themselves (see pages 34-5).

Farming in the 1920s had hardly changed since before the revolution. Only 3 per cent of agricultural land was owned by the state. The rest was divided into small farms run by peasants on their own behalf.

The agricultural community was divided. At the top were the **kulaks**, prosperous peasant farmers who made a good living for themselves. They were well-off and often employed other peasants to work their land. They could have bad harvests and not suffer too much. **Poor peasants** also owned their own land, but were much more affected by bad harvests. At the bottom of rural society were the **labouring peasants**, who sold their labour to farmers. They always suffered first and most severely when times were hard.

SOURCE A

Official government picture of peasants crowding to join a collective.

SOURCE B

'We are fifty to a hundred years behind the advanced countries. We must make up this gap in ten years. Either we do this or they crush us.'

Stalin's speech to the First Conference of Workers in 1931.

SOURCE C

'Whoever heard of such a thing – to give up our land and our cows and our tools and our buildings, to work all the time and divide everything with others? Nowadays members of the same family get in each other's way and quarrel and fight, and here we, strangers, are supposed to be like one family.'

From 'Red Bread' by Maurice Hindus, 1934. In 1929 Hindus returned to the village where he was born. This is his account of a peasant's view of collective farms, or 'Kolkhoz', as they were called.

SOURCE D

'Tell me, you wretched people, what hope is there for you if you remain on individual pieces of land? From year to year you divide and subdivide your strips of land. You cannot even use machinery on your land because no machine could stand the rough ridges that the strip system creates. Don't you see that there is nothing ahead of you but ruin and starvation?'

A Party official's view of the Kolkhoz, from M. Hindus, 'Red Bread', 1934.

SOURCE E

New farm machinery being made available to the collectives in the 1930s.

SOURCE F

'The countryside became the theatre of undeclared civil war. The peasants tenaciously clung to their property, attacked and killed party commissars, slaughtered cattle, burned barns and stables, and buried or destroyed whole harvests of grain. The [secret police] replied with mass executions and mass deportations. Mammoth concentration camps were set up in the enormous desolate plains of Siberia and in the icy wastes of the Far North.'

Isaac Deutscher, 'The Great Purges', broadcast in 1965.

By the late 1920s most peasants had enough to eat, and could have produced more food to help feed the growing town population. But if they did produce a surplus to sell to the towns, there was nothing to buy with the money they made. Few peasants could see any advantage to themselves in working harder to feed the towns, and so the problem grew.

Although the poorer peasants resented the kulaks, they did not want to see them abolished. Most of them simply hoped to be prosperous kulaks themselves one day. The ideal of working together for a 'common good', which included the interests of the workers in the towns, did not appeal to them. The peasants did not have the same enthusiasm for any of the Communist ideals which had fired the imaginations of the industrial workers. They were only interested in private ownership. Lenin had hoped to persuade the peasants to join collective, mechanized, farms. Stalin knew that Lenin's NEP was not working fast enough. He felt that the government could no longer afford to be patient with the peasants. Something had to be done urgently to meet the needs of industry and to bring the rural community into line with the rest of Soviet society.

The solution to these interrelated problems was found in the **collectivization of agriculture** programme. This coincided with the first of Stalin's Five-Year Plans for industry (see pages 44-5). Peasants were encouraged, and later forced, to join **collectives**. Their land and labour were pooled and all the members of the collective worked for the common good. Ninety per cent of each collective's produce was sold directly to the state for a fixed price. In return, the state made farm equipment available. The peasants' main source of income was now their share in the profits of the collective. Members of the collective kept their own houses, a small vegetable garden and a few tools and animals.

At first the government aimed to persuade the peasants through offering them incentives. Free housing and seed were given to the peasants to encourage them to join the collectives. Other facilities, like local hospitals, were also provided for the first time. These advantages were well publicized, but collectivization was still resisted. The kulaks had most to lose. Many of them deliberately sabotaged the first stages of collectivization by slaughtering livestock rather than giving them to the collective.

Eventually the government became more ruthless in order to speed up the process of collectivization. Now kulaks were evicted from their land and collectives were forcibly set up. Hatred of the kulaks as a class was encouraged, and kulaks were not allowed to join the collectives. Historians believe that many kulaks died while resisting eviction or by being sent to labour camps (see pages 40-1).

These harsher methods were successful. By 1935, 94 per cent of agricultural land had been collectivized and the kulak class had been eliminated. By 1939 the output of grain, meat and milk was much higher than in 1913. Stalin's policy worked, but the brutal way it was carried out led to lasting resentment. Although rural society had been revolutionized, the peasants were still sullen and unco-operative. In addition, many party members who approved of the idea of collectivization disliked the methods used to carry out the policy.

4.1 THE PERSECUTION OF THE KULAKS

EMPATHY

The kulaks were the richest peasant class. They owned their land, sometimes renting it out to other peasants. They often employed the poorer peasants to work their land for them. They were generally safe from the worst effects of bad harvests. Most other peasants envied the kulaks and hoped one day to be secure like them.

The Communist Party did not really know how to deal with the kulaks. They were the ablest of the peasant farmers, the people most likely to make a success of farming for the state. On the other hand, the kulaks were seen as the enemy of Communism because they were so successful as individuals.

Collectivization had always been the long-term aim of Communist economists. Most old Bolsheviks, including Lenin, believed that Communist ideas would spread naturally to the countryside. They thought that until most peasants wanted to join the collectives, collective farms would not work.

By 1929 the problem of supplying food to the growing towns was becoming critical. The peasants were not interested in producing more food than was necessary for their own basic needs, unless they could see some other advantages. They did not respond to government propaganda about the benefits of collectivization. As famine threatened again, Stalin introduced a policy of forced collectivization, and encouraged the destruction of the kulaks. Perhaps 5 million kulak families died in the labour camps between 1929 and 1936, and thousands more disappeared before reaching the camps. Anyone who tried to defend individuals was called a 'kulak-hireling' and suffered the same fate as the kulaks themselves.

Why were kulaks so vulnerable to this attack?

SOURCE C

A government poster of a kulak.

SOURCE A

'We have passed from the policy of restricting the exploiting tendencies of the kulaks to the policy of eliminating the kulaks as a class. To launch an offensive against the kulaks means we must strike at the kulaks, strike so hard as to prevent them from rising to their feet again.'

From a speech by Stalin in 1929.

SOURCE B

'Stock was slaughtered every night. Bulls, sheep, pigs, even cows were slaughtered, as well as calves for breeding. The dogs began to drag entrails about the village; cellars and barns were full with meat. "Kill, it's not ours any more", "Kill, they'll take it for meat anyway", "Kill, you won't get meat in the collectives" crept the insidious rumours. And they killed.'

From the novel 'Virgin Soil Upturned' by Mikhail Sholokov, 1931.

SOURCE D

'We are beginning seriously to re-equip agriculture. For this we must expand the development of collective and state farms. We must reinforce the support of the middle and poor peasant masses, as one of the means of breaking the reisitance of the kulaks and of obtaining from them the maximum grain surplus. This is necessary in order to be able to dispense with importing grain and to save foreign currency for the development of industry.'

From a speech by Stalin in 1929.

EMPATHY

SOURCE E

'In the background, guarded by the secret police with drawn revolvers, stood about twenty peasants, young and old, with bundles on their backs. A few of them were weeping. The others stood there sullen, resigned, helpless.

'I saw two militiamen leading a middle-aged peasant. His face was black and blue and his gait was painful. His clothes were ripped in a way indicating a struggle.'

V. Kravchenko, 'I Chose Freedom', 1932.

SOURCE F

A group of peasants carrying a banner with the inscription, 'We demand collectivization and the liquidization of the kulaks as a class', 1931.

SOURCE G

'Train loads of deported peasants left for the icy north, the forest, the steppes and the deserts. These were whole populations, who had lost everything; the old folk starved to death in mid-journey, new-born babies were buried on the banks of the roadside, and each wilderness had its crop of little crosses of white wood.'

Victor Serge, writing in 'Memoirs of a Revolutionary 1901-41', 1963.

EXERCISE

1 Scenes like the one described in Source E were repeated thousands of times throughout the Soviet Union. Why didn't the kulaks unite to resist the government policy?

2 a Why did the peasants act as they did in Source B?
  b What would a party member think of this kind of action?

3 Does Source F prove that some peasants were pleased to join the attack on the kulaks?

4 Stalin encouraged the persecution of the kulaks. Was this simply because he was a cruel man who liked the idea of people suffering?

4.2 THE LABOUR CAMPS

EVIDENCE

During the 1930s, huge labour camps were set up in remote parts of the USSR to house anyone who criticized Stalin's regime. This included the peasants who had resisted collectivization, Soviet citizens who had lived abroad, devout religious groups (especially the Jews), 'saboteurs', writers and university lecturers. The government claimed that these people were going to be re-educated through useful employment. This would benefit the whole of Soviet society and turn the prisoners into dedicated Communists.

The prisoners were put to work building roads and canals, mining, and working in industry and agriculture. This cheap labour force was one vital ingredient in the spectacular, if exaggerated, success of Stalin's Five-Year Plans.

Survivors give a very different impression of life in the labour camps. They claim that many thousands died and that thousands more suffered terribly in the harsh prisons.

What were conditions really like in the labour camps? What information do we need before we can make a realistic assessment of these conditions?

SOURCE A

These photographs were all taken from an official Soviet album celebrating the construction of the Belomor-Baltic Canal by political prisoners. The captions are translations from the original collection, published in 1934.

(a) Guns are held like this, not to frighten anyone, but just out of convenience.

◀ *(b) Labour will re-educate them.*

▲ *(c) We will teach Mother Nature a lesson, that's how we acquire our freedom.*

SOURCE B

Arrests and deaths in labour camps, 1937 – 8
Arrested   7,000,000
Died in camp   2,000,000

From Robert Conquest's, 'The Great Terror', 1968.

SOURCE C

'I managed somehow to eat my dinner. The quantity was enough to keep one starving to death, but the quality was such that it was difficult to stay alive.'

Eugenia Ginzburg was a University lecturer who spent eighteen years in prisons and labour camps. This extract is taken from her book 'Into the whirlwind', published in 1981.

SOURCE D

'It was one metre in width and less than two in length. An enormous latrine bucket without a cover and almost overflowing before my arrival stood in front of me with strings of wood lice over it and the walls. The floor was covered in human excrement. There was no air whatsoever, none, only unbearable stench stifling my throat. Breakfast was bread and a mug of very hot water to wash in and drink.'

Maria Joffe, a journalist who was imprisoned between 1929 and 1957. This is a description of solitary confinement.

SOURCE E

'At the end of the workday there were corpses left on the work site. The snow powdered their faces. At night the sledges went out and collected them. And in the summer bones remained from corpses which had not been removed in time, and together with the shingle they got into the concrete mixer. And in this way they got into the concrete of the last lock at the city of Belomorsk and will be preserved forever.'

From Alexander Solzhenitsyn's, 'The Gulag Archipelago', published in 1974.

SOURCE F

'The prisoner is isolated in a bare cell, containing one object only, a chamber-pot. He is usually put into a two-piece garb of untearable Terylene and perhaps given an indestructable sheet. On one occasion I saw a patient who had been put naked into the special cell. There is no furniture and during the day no mattress. He must eat his food either standing or off the floor.'

Dr Benjamin Lee on British prisoners isolated for their own protection, 'The Lancet', June 1983.

EXERCISE

1 a Source A is an official record of camp life. The photographs prove that conditions were reasonable for the inmates. Do you agree?
  b Source F is an official account of life in British prisons in the 1980s. Does it prove that British prisons are harsh places?
  c Sources C and D are accounts of prison life by ex-inmates who had reasons to hate Stalin. Their accounts cannot be reliable. Do you agree? Give reasons for your answer.
  d A source is only useful to a historian if it is reliable. Do you agree? Explain your answer.

2 In Source B, Robert Conquest provides a startling statistic about the death rate in the labour camps. Is this source useful on its own? What other information would make it more useful to a historian?

3 Source F is not about the Soviet Union at all. Can it help us to understand prison life in the Soviet Union?

4 a Solzhenitsyn is a novelist and a historian. He experienced life in the labour camps at first-hand. Source E is taken from a novel. How does that affect its reliability?
  b Why do you think Solzhenitsyn chose to write a novel rather than a history book?

4.3 SOVIET INDUSTRY AND THE FIVE-YEAR PLANS

Russia had not been a very advanced industrial power in 1914. The experience of the First World War, the loss of much industrial land and equipment to Germany after the Treaty of Brest-Litovsk, and then the Civil War, had seriously damaged the USSR's industrial development. The Soviet Union could not compete with the other industrial countries. These countries were still strongly opposed to Communism, and their industrial strength was one weapon they could use against the USSR. Lenin and Stalin knew that the economy had to be developed quickly to meet this threat.

At first Lenin had favoured self-governing workshops, where ordinary working people controlled their own factories. He soon realized that they did not know enough about production and marketing to do this successfully. The economic development of the Soviet Union could not be left to them alone. Lenin then set up the **State Planning Commission** (GOSPLAN) to guide the economic development of the USSR. The NEP allowed for some individual enterprise while the main industries remained firmly under state control (see pages 30-1).

The economic situation was not much better when Lenin died. The USSR was not an effective rival of the main industrial countries. It was clear that the problem was not simply an economic one – the attitudes of the working classes also needed changing if the USSR was to compete with other industrial countries. Different races within the Soviet Union had to learn to work together, and the lack of technological expertise in the workforce had to be overcome.

Soviet Industry and the Five-Year Plans

In 1928, under Stalin's direction, the **first Five-Year Plan** (1928-32) was produced by GOSPLAN, the State Planning Commission. The plan was a list of ambitious targets for the development of industry, power supply and transport. It emphasized the need for greater investment to create the basis for future wealth and expansion. Like all of the plans, it was closely related to the government's direction and control of agriculture.

Considerable progress had been made by 1933. At the Seventeenth Party Congress officials claimed that 'the Five-Year Plan has transformed Russia from an agricultural to an agricultural-industrial country: 57.5 per cent of the national income of the USSR has been derived from industry, transport and the building industry, and only 22.9 per cent of it comes from agriculture.'

The **second Five-Year Plan** (1933-8) had different goals. As collectivization of agriculture progressed, there was a great need for tractors. Output of tractors trebled in this period. The production of machinery, ball bearings and precision instruments, requiring skill and top-quality raw materials, was successfully encouraged in Moscow, Gorky and Leningrad. Water, road and rail transport were all improved. In a short space of time the USSR had become the world's third-greatest industrial power.

The production of consumer goods had not been a priority of the state planners before 1938. In the **third Five-Year Plan**, it was decided to produce 'luxuries' like radios, bicycles and household goods.

SOURCE A

'We must transform the USSR from a weak, agrarian country dependent upon the caprices of world capitalism, drive out the capitalist elements mercilessly, widen the front of the socialist forms of economy, create the economic basis for the construction of a socialist society, create in our country an industry which would be capable of re-equipping and organizing not only the whole of our industry but also of our transport and our agriculture on a socialist basis, create in the country all the necessary prerequisites for increasing to the utmost the defensive capacity of the country, enable it to organize determined resistance to any and every attempt at military intervention or military aggression from outside.'

Part of Stalin's speech introducing the first Five-Year Plan in 1928.

SOURCE B

The Dnieper Dam, almost complete in 1932, the pride of the first Five-Year Plan.

These things were taken for granted in other industrial countries. This policy changed when the threat of war with Germany meant that weapons had to be produced instead.

By the end of the 1930s the USSR was second only to the USA in its industrial production. This was a fantastic achievement for its people and its government. Huge new hydro-electric power stations were in operation. Massive new steel plants had been built and now produced top-quality steel which could be used in other new industries. Communications by road, rail and water had been transformed. Despite the sacrifices they had made, most industrial workers were justly proud of their country.

SOURCE   **E**

This machine showed people the progress of the first Five-Year Plan.

SOURCE   **C**

The production of farm machinery was increased. These tractors were leaving a new tractor factory in 1933.

SOURCE   **D**

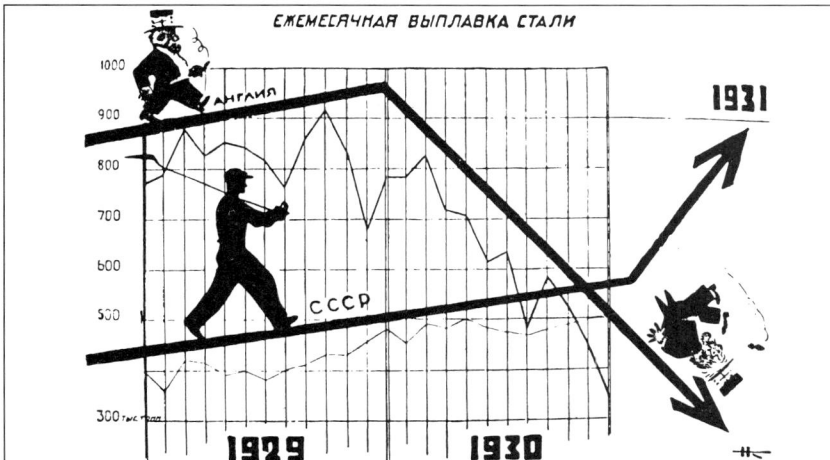

An official postcard celebrating Stalin's first Five-Year Plan.

QUESTIONS

1   Choose **one** phrase from the three given below which you think best summarizes Stalin's position, as outlined in Source A. Write the phrase down and then select extracts from the speech to support your answer.

- Stalin wanted to develop industry so there would be plenty of consumer goods to keep the Soviet citizens happy.

- Stalin wanted to develop industry so that it matched the achievements in agriculture.

- Stalin wanted to develop the whole economy to make the USSR safe from external threats.

4.4 THE PACE OF CHANGE

CHANGE

Few people recognized the Soviet Union's potential in the 1920s. The First World War and the Civil War had left the economy in a mess that most economists believed would take many years to put right. It was not only industrial and agricultural production and standards which needed to improve. The changes necessary to achieve such a transformation affected the whole of society. In particular, the attitudes of working people in the towns and countryside had to be changed in order to meet the targets set by Stalin and his advisers.

New industrial towns such as **Magnitogorsk** were quickly built from nothing and began to make a contribution to the economy. Thousands of people were resettled in new towns and given training. Old working habits were radically changed. Industrial life in the USSR would never be the same again. At first, working and living conditions in the industrial towns were at least as bad as they had been before the revolution, but gradually things improved. More and more facilities, such as shops, clubs, and hospitals, were provided.

In order to encourage people to work towards the targets set by the Five-Year Plans, workers who were very productive were made into heroes. They were given better pay, housing and conditions. The most famous of these workers was **Stakhanov**, a coal miner. He managed to cut fourteen more tonnes of coal in a shift by organizing his fellow workers. People who worked very hard on extra long shifts to improve production figures were called 'Stakhanovites' after him.

SOURCE A

'The pace must not be slackened! On the contrary, we must quicken it as much as is within our powers and possibilities. To slacken the pace would mean to lag behind, and those who lag behind are beaten. We are 50 or 100 years behind the advanced countries. We must make good this lag in 10 years. Either we do it or they will crush us.'

Stalin's 1931 speech explaining why he thought it was so urgent to modernize the USSR.

SOURCE B

'Within several years, half a billion cubic feet of excavation was done, 42 million cubic feet of reinforced concrete poured, five million tons of structural steel erected. This was done without sufficient labour, without necessary quantities of the most elementary supplies and materials. Brigades of young enthusiasts from every corner of the Soviet Union did the groundwork of railroad and dam construction necessary before work would begin on the plant itself. Later, groups of local peasants came to Magnitogorsk because of the bad conditions in the villages due to collectivization. Many were completely unfamiliar with industrial and processes. They had to start at the beginning and learn.'

J. Scott on the construction of Magnitogorsk, from 'Behind the Urals', 1942.

SOURCE C

'In early April it was still bitter cold, everything was still frozen solid. By May the city was swimming in mud. Bubonic plague had broken out not far from Magnitogorsk. The resistance of the population was very low because of undernourishment and consistent overwork. Sanitary conditions were appalling. By the middle of May the heat was intolerable. We were consumed by bed bugs and other vermin.'

J. Scott on working conditions in Magnitogorsk, from 'Behind the Urals', 1942.

SOURCE D

Soviet industrial production, 1928–37 (targets shown are in brackets)

	1927-8	1933	1937
Electricity (100m kWh)	5.1	13.4 (17.0)	36.2 (38.0)
Coal (m. tons)	35.4	64.3 (68.0)	128.0 (152.5)
Steel (m. tons)	4.0	5.9 (8.3)	17.7 (17.0)
Oil (m. tons)	11.7	21.4 (19.0)	28.5 (46.8)
Pig iron (m. tons)	3.3	6.2 (8.0)	14.5 (16.0)

SOURCE E

Poster showing a rich businessman mocking the first Five-Year Plan in 1928 and acknowledging its success in 1933.

SOURCE F

Sverdlovsk in the Urals in 1928.

SOURCE G

Sverdlovsk in 1933.

EXERCISE

1 a Draw a series of bar charts to show industrial development in the USSR between 1927 and 1937, using the information in Source D.

b Write a paragraph explaining the trends.

c Now mark in the targets set by Stalin for each industry.

d Did production levels ever match the targets?

e How significant do you think the general failure to meet the targets was?

2 The figures in Source D suggest that the years 1927 to 1933 were less productive than the years 1933 to 1937.
Why do you think this was?

3 Do the sources here help to explain the economic changes in the Soviet Union during the years 1927 to 1937? Explain your answer.

4 Do Sources F and G show **change**? Explain your answer.

5 Do Sources F and G show **progress**? Explain your answer.

4.5 THE OPPOSITION PURGES AND SHOW TRIALS

The decision to liquidate (get rid of) the kulaks early in the 1930s resulted in what has been described as an 'undeclared civil war'. The policy of taking the land from 24 million peasants and forcibly collectivizing it was resisted strongly, and then enforced with great brutality. Mass executions and deportations to huge concentration camps already tarnished Stalin's record on human rights. At the same time industrial development proceeded quickly, but did not bring much joy to the workers themselves. Stalin needed to encourage people to work for the future, in order to forget their present misery. Many ordinary people did respond to these appeals. They were encouraged by the impressive results of their work – for example by the new Dnieper Dam, and by promises of constitutional reform.

The new **constitution** announced by Stalin in 1936 was supposed to protect the civil liberties and democratic rights of Soviet citizens. Stalin's personal power was tremendous. He could not bear any challenges to his authority, and intended to keep his powerful position through a mixture of propaganda and terror.

SOURCE **B**

SOURCE **A**

Stalin signing a death warrant.

The caption to this cartoon reads: 'Visit the USSR's pyramids!' It was published by people who had fled the USSR during the Terror. The pyramids are formed from the skulls of those who died in the purges.

SOURCE C

Vyshinsky, Chief Prosecutor in the Moscow trials in 1937.

He set about **purging**, or getting rid of, people in the Communist Party who had opposed him in the past, or who might oppose him in the future. In 1934 a popular leading Communist, **Kirov**, was assassinated. Some historians believe that Stalin was partly responsible for the murder. Zinoviev, Kamenev and others were expelled from the party on the grounds that their past criticisms of Stalin might have influenced whoever it was who killed Kirov. Zinoviev and Kamenev were imprisoned, and Trotsky was denounced as the person who organized all these crimes. In the following months, thousands of so-called 'assassins of Kirov' were deported.

On 13 March 1936 the first of the great **show trials** was announced, and the **Terror** began in earnest. Sixteen 'old Bolsheviks' and heroes of the Civil War, including Zinoviev and Kamenev, were put on trial. They now faced charges of having been directly responsible for Kirov's death and of having plotted against Stalin and other members of the **Politburo** (the committee which ran the Communist Party). They all confessed to the crimes. The Chief Prosecutor concluded with the words 'I demand that the mad dogs be shot! Every one of them should be shot!' All sixteen were sentenced to death, and were executed on 24 August.

More trials were held. Many leaders of the party who seemed to be loyal Stalinists were found guilty of crimes against the country and against Stalin. They were condemned and executed. Thousands of party officials and administrators were shot, deported or simply replaced. Some 25,000 officers of the Red Army were removed. This had a very serious result, leaving the Red Army at a disadvantage on the eve of the Second World War. Leaders in every field were victims of the Terror, finding themselves denounced by friends, enemies and colleagues. Members of the **NKVD** (the secret police) who were not efficient enough in rounding up counter-revolutionaries, or who knew too much about the regime, were also killed or deported. The families of the accused people were considered equally guilty of crimes committed against the state, so wives, parents and children were deported too.

By the end of 1938 the Terror relaxed. Stalin had achieved his goal. He had purged the party of all rivals and opponents and stopped the development of any future critics. The cost of his intense suspicion in human terms was huge. The economy could not withstand further disruption and the international situation was increasingly threatening.

SOURCE D

'I should like to repeat that I am fully and utterly guilty. I am guilty of having been the organizer, second only to Trotsky, of that bloc whose chosen task was the killing of Stalin. I was the principal organizer of Kirov's assassination. The party saw where we were going and warned us, Stalin warned us scores of times, but we did not heed these warnings. We entered into alliance with Trotsky.'

Part of Zinoviev's last plea at his show trial.

4.6 SILENCING THE OPPOSITION

EMPATHY

The social and political range of Stalin's victims was wide. They included party members of all ranks; police and military personnel; citizens who were accused of dealing with foreigners and were called spies; and the friends and relatives of all the above. The numbers involved were staggering. Tens of thousands of 'enemies of the people' were sent to concentration camps; thousands more were executed following public or secret trials. Why didn't anyone speak out against the purges, or why did they have little effect if they did?

SOURCE A

Tukhachevsky (far left on bottom row), Deputy Commissar of Defence and the ablest Red Army Commander, reviewing the May Day Parade with Stalin in 1937. Twelve days later he was accused of leading a Trotskyist plot against Stalin. He was tried and executed.

SOURCE B

'My whole case, dear [Stalin], is a typical example of provocation, slander and violation of elementary justice. I shall now touch upon the one really disgraceful act of my life, my confession in which I admitted to counter-revolutionary activity. I was unable to endure the tortures to which Usakov subjected me. He tortured me even while my broken ribs were causing me agony. He forced me to accuse myself and others. He dictated to me most of my confession.'

Part of a letter to Stalin, written from prison by Eikhe, the former party leader in Siberia.

SOURCE C

'I should have addressed this letter to you much earlier, when Zinoviev and Kamenev were executed. But I was silent then, I did not raise my voice in protest, for this I bear grave responsibility. He who still remains silent becomes Stalin's accomplice – and a traitor to the working class and to socialism. I am sending back the Order of the Red Banner. To wear it now, when so many hangmen are wearing it, would be beneath my dignity.'

Letter of resignation from Reiss, Chief of the European Network of Soviet Counter-Intelligence, 18 July 1937. Six weeks later he was murdered.

SOURCE D

'With bated breath the people in the shanties listened to the creaking of the snow under the feet of those who were marched away. All sounds had already died down, yet everyone was still listening tensely. After about an hour shots resounded across the tundra. The crowd in the shanties knew what awaited them, but after the long hunger strike of the previous year, and many more months of freezing and starvation, they had not the strength to resist.'

An account of an execution in the Vorkuta concentration camps of the far north. It appeared in a Menshevik paper for people who had fled the country, and was signed 'M.B.'

SOURCE E

'The Murderer's Hygiene' – a caricature of Trotsky from 1937. The verse beneath the cartoon reads: 'The hero of crimes and treachery, does not forget the rules of hygiene. Those who are in the pay of fascists, live by scientific rules. The executioner, finishing his day's work, washes his hands in fear.'

SOURCE F

'Pyatakov (Deputy Commissar of Heavy Industry) confessed that in December 1935 he had gone by plane from Berlin to Oslo, where he was to obtain instructions from Trotsky. The authorities of the Oslo airport, however, issued a statement declaring that no plane coming from Berlin had landed at the airport in December 1935 or for many weeks before or after that date.'

Isaac Deutscher, 'The Great Purges', broadcast in 1965.

SOURCE G

The Soviet Ambassador in Oslo made an official objection to the asylum granted to Trotsky by the Norwegian government on 29 August 1936. 'My colleagues in the government were afraid of economic reprisals. I was against the proposal that we should intern Trotsky. But I was outvoted by my colleagues in the cabinet. For five months Trotsky was forbidden to communicate with the outside world.'

Koht, Norway's Foreign Minister, in 1936.

SOURCE H

'Every Bolshevik, every worker, every citizen of our Soviet land is clearly aware that, if we have been able to rout all these fascist agents, all these contemptible Trotskyists, Bukharinists and bourgeois nationalists, we are indebted to our great leader, our great and glorious Stalin.'

Extract from a speech given by Nikita Khrushchev, Stalin's later successor, to the Eighteenth Party Congress in March 1939.

SOURCE I

'The accusations levelled against the defendants and myself are not only false – they represent the greatest frame-up in history.'

Statement made by Trotsky, from exile in Norway, as the Moscow trials of 1936 began.

SOURCE J

'Whoever was critical of any concept of Stalin's was doomed to moral and physical annihilation.'

Khrushchev at the Twentieth Party Congress in 1956.

EXERCISE

1 Study Sources E, G and I. What effect would Trotsky's silence have had on ordinary Soviet citizens following the trials?

2 Why didn't people like Eikhe (Source B) speak out against the purges before they fell victim to them?

3 What effect would Eikhe's confession have had on the people who read about the trials in the Soviet press?

4 How do you think ordinary people in the Soviet Union felt about the trials and about the execution of so many people who had once been heroes of the revolution?

4.7 WHO WAS THE REAL LEON TROTSKY?

EVIDENCE

Trotsky was one of the leaders of the Bolshevik revolution of 1917, and he played a vital role in Soviet history until 1924. His reputation has always been the subject of great controversy.

Trotsky's opposition to Stalin led to his expulsion from the Communist Party and to permanent exile from Russia in 1928. During the purges Trotsky, who was in exile at the time, was accused of being a Nazi collaborator. Many of Trotsky's former political allies were tried and executed on the grounds that they had collaborated with him. Even some of his former enemies found themselves admitting to crimes involving Trotsky. He tried to defend himself, and those facing execution in the USSR. He constantly criticized Stalin's way of governing. Hardly anyone in the USSR heard Trotsky's denial of the charges against him. Trotsky's sympathizers held a public meeting, called the **Mexico Inquiry**, to discuss the

SOURCE B

A Soviet cartoon published in March 1938, showing Trotsky and other anti-Stalinists dining courtesy of the Gestapo.

SOURCE A

The Bolshevik Central Committee of 1917, produced in 1927.

SOURCE C

'In the trials there figured no fighters, no conspirators, but only puppets in the hands of the secret police. They played assigned roles. The aim of the disgraceful performance? To eliminate the whole opposition; to poison the very source of critical thought, to confirm Stalin's totalitarian regime.'

Trotsky's analysis of the Moscow trials, from a speech made at the Mexico Inquiry.

charges against him. Stalin was angered by the reports he received about Trotsky, and he arranged his death in August 1940.

Trying to assess Trotsky's role in history is a difficult task because there are so many powerful and conflicting images of him. For example, most Russians who were subjected to Stalinist propaganda believe that Trotsky was an enemy of Communism, even that he was a fascist collaborator. Outside the USSR, many people in the West think of Trotsky as the worst kind of Communist, because he wanted to spread the revolution throughout the world.

SOURCE D

ЦЕНТРАЛЬНЫЙ КОМИТЕТ, ИЗБРАННЫЙ НА VI СЪЕЗДЕ РСДРП (БОЛЬШЕВИКОВ):

◀ *The Bolshevik Central Committee of 1917, produced in 1935.*

EXERCISE

1 Are Sources A and D primary or secondary?

2 Would a historian studying Trotsky find Sources A and D useful? Give reasons for your answer.

3 Source B shows Trotsky as a Nazi collaborator. In fact Trotsky was always opposed to the Nazis. Does this mean that historians will not find this a useful source?

4 Trotsky made the speech in Source C to clear his name. Does this affect the reliability of this source?

5 There was only one real Trotsky. Careful research by historians can provide a balanced and accurate view of his life and ideas. The real Trotsky had little influence over events in the USSR or the world after 1924. Inaccurate images of Trotsky have had much more impact. Which do you think is more important for a historan to understand, the 'real' Trotsky or the images of Trotsky? Explain your answer.

5.1 SOVIET FOREIGN POLICY, 1917–41

We have already seen that foreign policy and domestic policy were closely related in the USSR. Stalin constantly referred to external threats and dangers when urging the modernization of Soviet agriculture and industry. In this chapter we will see how serious those dangers really were.

Communism was not popular with other European powers. The Bolshevik revolution in October 1917 had taken Russia out of the First World War. Russia's former allies felt abandoned. The Western powers tried hard to defeat the Reds, hoping that if the Tsar returned to power Russia would come back into the war against Germany. The new Communist government argued that national barriers were not important, and that ordinary people should unite to bring about world revolution. The Communists were therefore regarded with a great deal of suspicion by the world outside.

In 1919 the **Comintern** was set up. It aimed to promote Communism in other countries through close links with the Soviet Union. The host countries were deeply suspicious of the Comintern's activities, believing that it would encourage revolution. In 1920 the Red Army invaded Poland as the first stage of the plan to achieve world revolution. Once the Reds had been crushingly defeated in the **Battle of the Vistula**, most of the Soviet leadership believed that world revolution was something that would happen in the future. In the meantime peace with the Soviet Union's neighbours was desirable.

After Lenin's death, Trotsky continued to preach the idea of a **permanent revolution** and the defeat of world capitalism. These were traditional Communist ideas. Meanwhile Stalin began to develop the idea of **socialism in one country**. This policy was a practical response to the USSR's problems. Stalin abandoned traditional attitudes. He knew that the USSR could not fight the Western powers and hope to win. He had to give the Five-Year Plans time to work so that the country could build up its fighting forces. Peace was essential until this was achieved. He therefore argued that a Communist country could live in peace with its capitalist neighbours. Instead of encouraging revolutions elsewhere, Stalin tried to get on with the USSR's neighbours. Litvinov, Commissar for Foreign Affairs, made alliances in Eastern Europe which helped to strengthen the Soviet Union.

In the 1930s Stalin's foreign policy was designed to avoid confrontation and to maintain Soviet security. Three examples of Soviet diplomacy illustrate this.

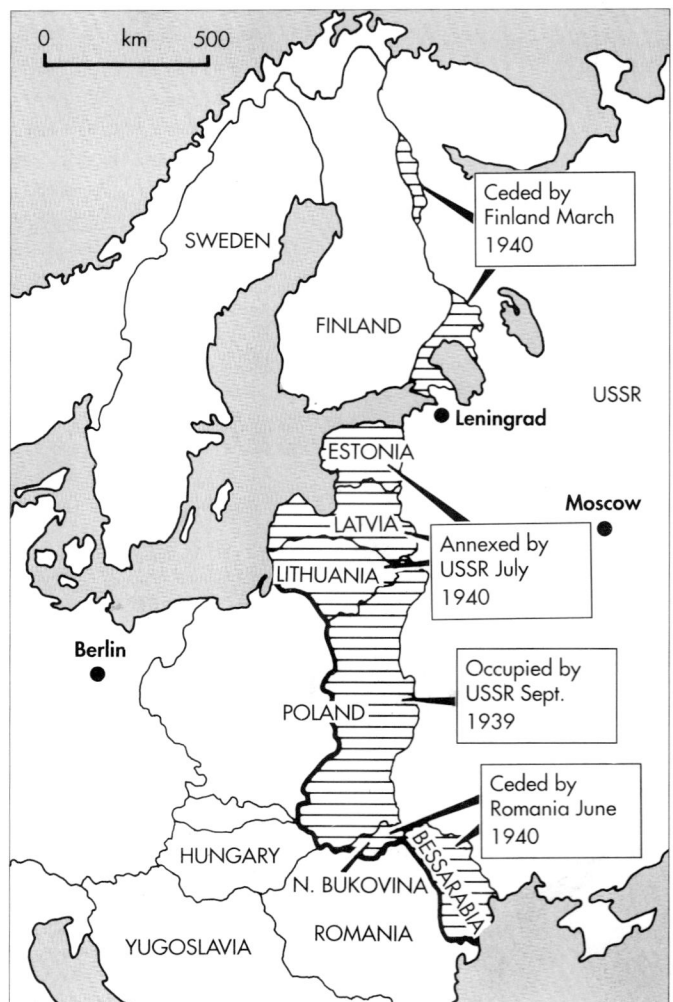

Stalin wanted to create a 'buffer zone' between Germany and the USSR. This map shows Soviet expansion, 1939 – 40.

In 1931 the Japanese invaded **Manchuria**, an area in which the USSR had been increasing its influence. The invasion threatened the safe frontier that the Soviet Union had spent years building up in the region. The Japanese were prepared to fight, despite protests at the League of Nations. Some Red Army generals were anxious to defend the USSR's rights in Manchuria, but Stalin preferred to retreat. Litvinov sold the Russian-owned railway in Manchuria to the Japanese. Stalin was more convinced than ever of the need to reform and expand the Red Army.

The rise of **Hitler and the Nazi Party** in Germany posed a more menacing threat to Soviet security. Hitler had well-advertised ambitions to defeat Communism and to gain territory or 'breathing space' for the new Reich. Stalin's attitude towards Germany in the 1930s shows his practical political skills. He tried to negotiate with Hitler throughout the decade. In case these talks should break down he also supported the idea of collective security, negotiating with France and Great Britain.

The **Spanish Civil War** (1936–8) is a good example of the USSR's complex foreign policy. Hitler was helping the Fascists in Spain. The Republicans were the USSR's natural allies in the Civil War, but Stalin could not afford to offend Hitler by supporting them strongly. Large-scale Soviet intervention in Spain would also have awakened the old fears about international revolution which still haunted Britain and France. The Fascists won.

When Germany and Japan signed an **Anti-Comintern Pact**, Stalin was convinced of the need for an alliance with Britain and France. Litvinov tried harder than ever to make collective security a reality. Western Europe remained doubtful of Soviet intentions, and tried to calm Hitler by accepting the German occupation of Czechoslovakia in the **Munich Agreement** of 1938.

Hitler immediately began preparations for an invasion of **Poland**. Stalin felt that Soviet safety was seriously threatened. When Stalin failed to form an alliance with Britain and France he replaced Litvinov with the more pro-Nazi Molotov and made a **Non-Aggression Pact** with Germany. In September 1939 Germany and the USSR jointly invaded Poland.

Stalin still thought that it was important to improve his defences against Hitler. In November 1939 the Red Army invaded Finland. This was an attempt to gain strategic sites for the defence of Leningrad. The huge number of Soviet casualties, together with the anger of Western powers, forced the USSR to make peace in March 1940. More buffers were gained in 1940 when the USSR forcibly annexed the Baltic states of Latvia, Estonia and Lithuania, Bessarabia and Romanian Bukovina, taking advantage of Germany's preoccupation with the war against France.

Stalin's foreign policy had largely been determined by the need to keep the Germans happy and to withstand the Nazi threat. He was surprised and disappointed by the German invasion of Soviet territory in June 1941.

Manchuria: the Japanese and Soviet interests.

SOURCE A

'The Russia of today, – deprived of its Germanic ruling class, is not a possible ally in the struggle for German liberty. A Russo-German coalition would be catastrophic for us.

'It must never be forgotten that the present rulers of Russia are blood-stained criminals, that here we have the dregs of humanity which overran a great state, degraded and extirpated millions of educated people out of sheer blood-lust and which now for nearly ten years have ruled with such a savage tyranny as was never known before.'

Adolf Hitler, 'Mein Kampf', written in 1924.

CAUSATION

5.2 THE NAZI – SOVIET PACT

In 1938 Hitler demanded large areas of Czechoslovakia. The USSR and France had both signed treaties saying they would help defend the Czechs if they were attacked. Neither did. At the **Munich Conference** Britain, France, Germany and Italy agreed that Hitler could take the land he wanted. The Czech government had no choice but to agree.

The USSR had not done anything to defend the Czechs. The USSR had also been left out of the Conference. Stalin saw this as dangerous isolation. If the other Great Powers got into the habit of meeting and making decisions they might make some which hurt the USSR. The **Munich crisis**, as it was called, showed Stalin the USSR needed an ally.

At Munich, Hitler said that the Czech land he wanted was his 'last territorial demand in Europe'. This did not last long. On 15 March 1939, German troops took over the rest of Czechoslovakia. Six days later Hitler demanded part of Poland.

In April 1939 Stalin suggested an alliance between Britain and France, and the USSR. The three powers would agree to defend each other against a possible German attack. Britain and France said no. The British and French leaders felt they could not trust Stalin. To them he was a dictator just as ruthless as Hitler, and a Communist.

Stalin may well have felt he could not trust Britain and France. Since Hitler came to power they had done nothing but give in to all of his demands. They might give in again over Poland.

ACTIVITIES

1 a Look at Source A. What are Stalin and Hitler standing over?
 b What is the cartoonist's view about the Nazi-Soviet Pact?
 c Is the date of the cartoon significant?

2 a Source B suggests another motive for the Nazi-Soviet Pact. What is it?
 b What impression of the Nazi-Soviet Pact is the cartoonist trying to give?

3 Which do you think is more reliable, source C or Source D? Give reasons for your answer.

SOURCE A

Cartoon by David Low, 'Evening Standard', 2 September 1939.

SOURCE B

Cartoon by David Low, 'Evening Standard', 4 November 1939.

August – September 1939

During August Hitler's demands for part of Poland grew. Germany and the USSR began secret talks about a pact between themselves. In August Britain and France changed their minds and suggested an alliance to Stalin. On 23 August the **Nazi-Soviet Non-Aggression Pact** was signed. This was a considerable shock to the rest of the world. Communism and Fascism were opposites. Hitler and Stalin usually claimed each was the only person who could save Europe from the other. Yet here they were making an alliance.

Events moved quickly after the Pact was signed. Britain and France said they would defend Poland, but Poland was too far away from them to get help there in time. Only the USSR could have helped Poland and the USSR had signed a public treaty saying it would not fight Germany. On 1 September German troops invaded Poland. On 3 September Britain and France declared war on Germany. The Second World War in Europe had begun.

SOURCE C

'Usually when Western sources discuss the Nazi-Soviet Pact they raise the question of an alleged **Secret Protocol**. This story is not new. The Soviet Chief Prosecutor at the Nuremberg War Trials labelled it a forgery, and correctly so. His declaration was a challenge to all those who wished to believe the forgery. After all, he made his statement right in front of Hitler's Foreign Minister, Ribbentrop, sitting there in the dock. It is well known that lies spread quickly.'

Andrei Gromyko, 'Memories', 1989. Gromyko was Foreign Minister for thirty years from 1957. In 1939 he was Ambassador to the United States and trusted by Stalin.

SOURCE D

NEW PROOF OF PACT BETWEEN HITLER AND STALIN

Proof from the Soviet archives that the USSR did conclude a secret agreement with Nazi Germany in 1939 has been published in a Moscow journal.

The Agreement allowed the USSR to invade eastern Poland, attack Finland, and occupy the Baltic States. Its text was published in the West 40 years ago when a copy was found in the archives of the German Foreign Ministry. Until last year the Soviet authorities refused to discuss the existence of such an agreement. A special Commission of the Congress of People's Deputies is investigating whether there was a secret deal with Hitler. This move follows a recent report by Soviet and Polish historians in the official communist newspaper, **Pravda**, which said that a secret agreement was concluded.

◀ *The Guardian, July 1989.*

Events August – November 1939

12 August
British and French arrive for talks in Moscow.

23 August
Nazi-Soviet Pact signed.

1 September
Germany invades Poland.

3 September
Britain and France declare war on Germany.

17 September
USSR invades east Poland.

27 September
Poland surrenders, divided between Germany and USSR.

30 November
USSR invades Finland.

EXERCISE

1 The Munich Conference did not involve the USSR. Does this mean it cannot have been a cause of the Nazi-Soviet Pact? Explain your answer.

2 What motives might Stalin have had for a pact with the Nazis?

3 What motives might Hitler have had for a pact with the USSR?

4 a Do you think either Hitler or Stalin signed the Pact in order to start the Second World War?
  b Does this mean the Nazi-Soviet Pact was not one of the causes of the Second World War?

5.3 THE USSR AT WAR, 1941–45

Despite Hitler's constant and well-publicized promises to defeat Communism, Stalin believed that he had won a breathing-space for the USSR by the Non-Aggression Pact and the joint invasion of Poland in 1939. In 1940 the Germans seemed to be concentrating on their western frontier. No one thought that they would take on the Communists in the east at the same time. Stalin believed Hitler would be bound by the Nazi-Soviet Pact until 1942.

The huge German invasion of the USSR in 1941 therefore took Stalin by surprise. German armies advanced rapidly on Leningrad and Moscow, and through the Ukraine. Stalin called for a policy of **scorched earth**: the deliberate destruction of everything that might otherwise help the invaders. This marked the beginning of the enormous sacrifices made by all Soviet citizens in their struggle to defeat Fascism and to defend their country. The photographs in this Unit show something of their suffering and their courage.

It was now clear that the modernization programme, which had been ruthlessly undertaken at great personal cost to millions of Soviet citizens, had been essential for Soviet survival. The USSR which Lenin had led could not have withstood this determined invasion by the Germans. Stalin's pre-war foreign policy also seems more justifiable with hindsight. The Nazis were successful in their 1941 offensive, and only years of desperate struggle freed the USSR. If Stalin had not tried to negotiate with Hitler in 1939, the invasion might have taken place earlier, when the USSR was even less prepared. The defeat of Fascism would then have been even less certain.

SOURCE B

The battle for Stalingrad, 1942.

SOURCE C

German soldiers entering a Soviet town, burnt down as its citizens left. Stalin ordered people to destroy anything which might be useful to the Nazis. This was known as the 'scorched earth' policy.

SOURCE A

Soviet women being given military training during the 1930s.

The map shows the extent of Soviet territorial losses during 1941. The land lost was industrially advanced, with a huge population, an enormous amount of arable land and railways. The Germans pressed on towards Moscow. The winter of 1941–2 was a bitter one, and gave the Soviet army a chance to fight back. In 1942 the Germans continued to do well, but they were fighting on too many fronts. The battle for **Stalingrad** was fought at tremendous cost, but ended in a Soviet victory. Hitler's defeat here was a turning point in the war. In the summer of 1943 the Germans attacked again, but this offensive was not successful. From this time the Soviets and their allies were defeating the Germans. April and May of 1945 saw the last battle in Europe when Berlin was taken. The USSR then joined the coalition against Japan. But Soviet soldiers did not fight – the war was brought to an abrupt end by the use of the atomic bomb.

At least 20 million Soviet citizens died during the war. Millions more were permanently disabled. The cities, towns and countryside of the European part of the Soviet Union had been devastated. Some 25 million people were homeless. These sacrifices had been made to free the USSR. Soviet citizens now had very high expectations of the peace.

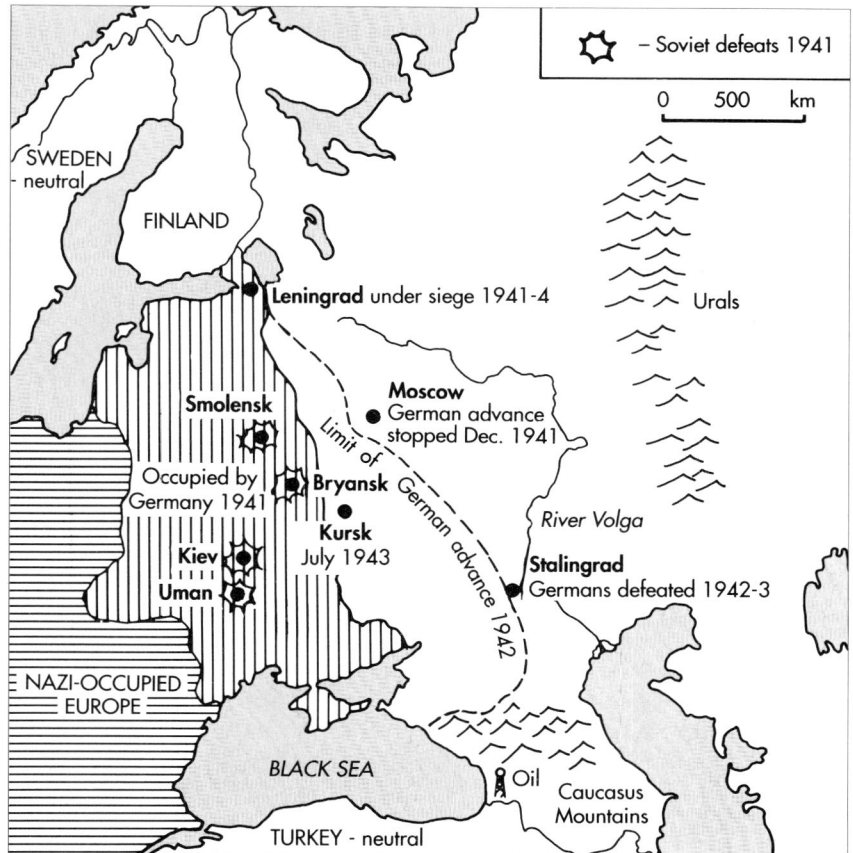

The Soviet Union's War.

5.4 STALIN'S LAST YEARS, 1945–53

CHANGE

The destruction of agricultural land, industrial buildings, housing, transport and people during the war had been enormous. Stalin was anxious to get on with the reconstruction of the Soviet Union, and introduced the **fourth Five-Year Plan** (1946–50). The challenge of rebuilding the economy was met by the industrial workers – by 1948 output levels matched, and sometimes exceeded, pre-war levels. Agricultural workers did not react so enthusiastically, and agriculture remains a serious economic problem in the Soviet Union.

SOURCE A

Reconstruction in the Soviet Union.

SOURCE B

'The main tasks of the new Five-Year Plan are to restore the afflicted districts of the country, to restore industry and agriculture to their pre-war level and then to exceed this level to a more or less considerable degree. Not to mention the fact that the ration card system will be abolished in the near future, special attention will be given to consumer goods, to raising the standard of living of the working people by means of the steady reduction of the prices of all commodities and to extensive construction of scientific research institutes of all kinds which will enable science to deploy its forces.

'As to plans for a longer period, our party intends to organize a new powerful upsurge of the national economy which would enable us, for instance, to raise the level of our industry three-fold compared with the pre-war level.

'Only under such conditions can we regard our country as guaranteed against any accidents.'

Stalin's speech introducing the fourth Five-Year Plan, 1946.

SOURCE C

Stalin in his last years.

Stalin's determination to keep supreme control, and his paranoia about the development of other ideas and policies, became even more noticeable in his last years. He still exercised tight control over the Communist Party, and execution or removal of those whom Stalin believed might challenge his position was not uncommon. There is even some evidence which suggests that Stalin was moving towards another purge of the party shortly before his death.

After the war, Soviet anxieties about hostile foreign powers meant that the policy of 'socialism in one country' no longer seemed appropriate. Stalin now created satellite states around the USSR to protect the country from a future invasion from the West. For example, the liberation of Romania, Bulgaria and Yugoslavia gave Stalin the opportunity to impose revolution in these countries by setting up Communist Provisional Governments. Economic links soon bound the satellite states of Eastern Europe to the Soviet Union.

The war-time co-operation between the Allies – the USSR, the United States and Great Britain – vanished within eight years. Mutual suspicion and mistrust brought about the division of Europe, and the beginning of the **cold war**.

EXERCISE

1 Pick out two phrases from Source B; one which shows that Stalin wanted to reward the Soviet citizens for their efforts during the war, and another which shows that he would still require a huge effort and sacrifice from them. Explain both aspects of his policy in your own words.

2 Having studied events in the USSR throughout Stalin's career, try to assess how and why attitudes towards him varied even while he was still alive.

    a Complete the following table:

	Attitudes towards Stalin in:			
	1924	1939	1945	1950
British diplomat				
Soviet peasant				
Soviet labourer				
Communist Party member				

    b Look at each person's reaction to Stalin from 1924 to 1950. Why did individuals' attitudes towards Stalin change over time?

    c Look at each year in turn. Explain why there were differences in the ways in which people reacted to Stalin at any one time.

    d Choose one example from the chart where you think that there would have been a difference between what an individual thought about Stalin and what that individual was willing to say about Stalin publicly. Explain your choice.

5.5 DESTROYING OR RECREATING STALIN'S LEGEND

CAUSATION

In pages 32-3 you saw how Stalin worked hard to create a public image of himself as a father of the revolution and of the peoples of the USSR. Stalinists contributed to this image-making in their speeches and writings.

During the thirty years of Stalin's rule, the USSR experienced enormous upheavals. You have been able to measure and assess the Soviet Union's record of economic, social and political change. It can be argued that these were essential for the survival of the Soviet state. However, the cost in human terms of all these changes was very high. Many groups and individuals, from the kulaks to important political rivals, suffered terribly in Stalin's Soviet Union. After the purges very few people spoke out against Stalin. Yet since his death many, including his former ally and successor **Khrushchev**, have condemned him. One historian, Isaac Deutscher, suggests a reason why people did not criticize Stalin before his death: 'His closest lieutenants lived in constant fear of him, hovering ceaselessly between life and death.' How adequate is this explanation of the lack of criticism?

A programme of **'de-Stalinization'** has been undertaken in the USSR in an effort to discredit Stalin and to disassociate others from the brutal aspects of his regime. It was easy to turn the 'cult of personality', the devotion to Stalin, on its head – Stalin was now to be blamed for all the outrages of the previous thirty years.

SOURCE B

'Comrades we have been pursuing our struggle under the guidance of a leader of genius, of our great teacher, our glorious Stalin. We have been pursuing this struggle against all the enemies of the people. Glory to our great Stalin.'

Part of a speech delivered by Khrushchev in 1952.

SOURCE C

'Nero too was, like Stalin, the product of his age. Yet when he perished his statues were smashed and his name was everywhere effaced. The vengeance of history is more powerful than the most powerful General Secretary. I venture to think this is consoling.'

Extract from a book on Stalin by Trotsky, found after his assassination in 1940.

SOURCE A

Part of a May Day celebration in 1952.

SOURCE D

'Comrades, Stalin's acts were not the outcome of persuasion, nor of patient co-operation with people. He imposed his ideas. He demanded absolute submission. Whoever was critical of any concept of Stalin's was doomed to moral and physical annihilation.'

Khrushchev at the Twentieth Party Congress in 1956.

CAUSATION

Stalin lying in state in Moscow in March 1953. Khrushchev and others are paying their respects.

SOURCE **F**

Crowds observing three minutes' silence for Stalin in March 1953.

SOURCE **G**

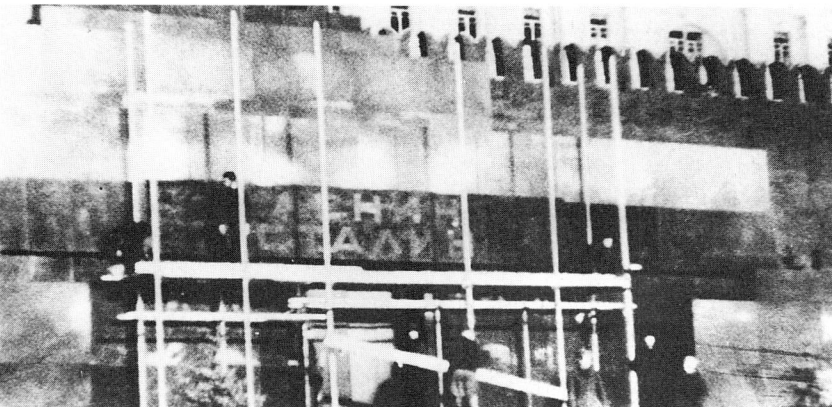

Stalin's body is removed from Lenin's mausoleum in Red Square, October 1961.

EXERCISE

1 For each source:
  a say whether it is primary or secondary.
  b try to work out whose attitudes towards Stalin are being expressed.

2 What do Sources A, B, E and F show about attitudes towards Stalin before his death?

3 What do Sources C, D and G show about attitudes towards Stalin?

4 Do you consider either group of sources to be a more reliable source of information than the other? Give reasons for your answer.

5 Do you think one group of sources is more useful than the other? Give reasons for your answer.

INDEX